Embraced:
Many Stories, One Destiny

Tharsten

May the God of hope
embrace your life
now & forever

Mark French Buchanan

Embraced:
Many Stories, One Destiny

You, Me,
and Moltmann

Mark French Buchanan

Foreword by
Jürgen Moltmann

WIPF & STOCK · Eugene, Oregon

EMBRACED
Many Stories, One Destiny

Wipf & Stock
An Imprint of Wipf and Stock Publishers
199 W. 8th Ave., Suite 3
Eugene, OR 97401

www.wipfandstock.com

ISBN 13: 978-1-4982-2921-0

Manufactured in the U.S.A.

To my children
May the way of hope
guide your journey

Contents

Foreword

I LIKE ORIGINAL IDEAS.

Pastor Mark Buchanan had an exceptional idea—to tell theology through real life stories. The great model is Martin Buber. Buber told his Jewish-Cabalistic theology of the Shekinah, the indwelling of the God of Israel in his stories of the Chasidim, the Jewish communities in Eastern Europe. Mark Buchanan too tells stories of the indwelling, life-giving love of the God of Jesus Christ. They are not stories of success, but stories of consolation. "Where I am empty, here I have found God resides" is how Pastor Buchanan expressed it in his letter to me.

I have often asked myself whether my change from the pastorate to a professorship was right. From a world of lived theology, I came into an academic world of teaching theology and there remained. Whenever I climb up a pulpit to preach a sermon and look out at the listening congregation, the pastor in me rises up and is lured out of the one-colored academic world into the rich and colorful life of the congregation of Christ. It is in those times that I wish I would have stayed as a pastor in the midst of a Christian community. Mark Buchanan has touched a hidden side in my personality.

Reading his book I have learned from his life experience, his wisdom, and his sense of humor. With theology life grows richer and more exciting, because Christian faith is not only a listening and trusting heart, but a life-community with Jesus Christ. We study theology not only with our minds but also with our life and death experiences. Mark Buchanan has also integrated my own life and death experiences in his stories. If my experiences are a witness to the One "who crowneth you with loving kindness and tender mercies" (Ps 103:4), then that is alright with me.

The attentive reader of this book will discover the traces of the *embrace* of God's life-giving love in his or her own life, for truly we are surrounded by divine presence just as we are surrounded by the air that we breathe.

Jürgen Moltmann
Tubingen
August 15, 2015

Acknowledgments

NONE OF US DETERMINE our own destiny. As God's favor finds us, God's destiny determines our future. God gathers from within and around us everything, including all that ends in naught, and in the words of the Apostle Paul, makes "all things work together for good" (Rom 8:28). Jürgen Moltmann's insights describe this gathering—which is drawn together through death on a cross and bursts forth in one shared destiny—as God's.

I wrote this book to share the wonder of such a destiny. The writing has shown me that this same wonder is woven into each step that every one of us takes. In reviewing the decades of reflection and.years of writing I am struck that the direction of my own journey was greatly influenced by fellow travelers.

My journey into hope began in earnest under the guidance of Dr. J. Christiaan Beker. My professor and friend led me into the mystery of finding strength in weakness. His words triumphantly continue to echo throughout my life especially in times of despair and remorse. "The victory of the gospel is that of the grace of God in Christ that contradicts the world and our own strength, and yet establishes beachheads of God's dawning new world in the midst of the old world."[1] Dr. Beker's beckoning drew me out of the landing craft and onto the shores of the new creation. There he concluded, "Thus, in the light of

---

1. Beker, *Paul the Apostle*, 301.

hope that groans for the victory of the new age, victory in this life is comfort in the midst of suffering and grace and power in the midst of weakness."[2] It was Dr. Beker who introduced me to Dr. Moltmann and whispered the interpretive key to Dr. Moltmann's writings—"suffering."

Through scores of Moltmann's thick tomes of theology I found hope, just as my professor had taught me, in the groaning of the world. What Moltmann's theology did was to indwell hope in me and on a grand scale point to hope that encompasses all things. After decades of trudging paths that led out into the world and others that led inward, I discovered there was "an interpenetration" of hope.[3] God's hope rising up and descending within me sparked the gift of God's shared life in me. I am profoundly grateful for the hope of ever-new life that the progression of Moltmann's theology has placed in me and in my union with the world.

It was Dr. Moltmann's encouragement that kept me writing, but it was my editor Virginia Christman who fashioned every chapter, paragraph and sentence into a cohesive whole. She changed my voice from passive to active, disciplined my descriptions and fought for clarity in every one of my theological explanations. Yet what I am most thankful for is Virginia's determination to make theology accessible to the hopeless, the suffering and the dying as more than just a testimony but the gift of hope that leads to everlasting life.

I am indebted to the generosity of Dr. Matthew Lundberg of Calvin College. He spontaneously accepted my request to coach me in theological thinking and writing. The urging of the Holy Spirit sent me out onto the Calvin College campus trusting that my steps would be guided. I discovered Dr. Lundberg's office door ajar. The opening was just enough for the Spirit to quicken our relationship and subsequently shower me with the benefit of Dr. Lundberg's theological insight and well-honed writing skills.

2. Ibid., 302.

3. Moltmann, *Coming of God*, 278.

ACKNOWLEDGMENTS

I am most grateful for the support that my wife, Susan, has given me through patience, diligent first editing and endless punctuation lessons. However this is not what anchors the joy I have in sharing the venture of writing with her. In the midst of parenting, balancing careers and serving in the life of the church, Susan lives the theology I struggle to express. For me she has forged the path and at times taken my hand and led me to where both God's hope and holiness is found. Her inclusion of my journey models for me the embrace of God. Our shared journey has given me hope that I with others am walking the wondrous way that leads to union with God.

Introduction

IT IS A JOY for me to testify to the hope that so faithfully beckons me ahead. I am grateful for the embrace of God, which draws people together and wondrously links their futures to his own. As I looked forward to compiling this book of stories, I also looked back on a single event in 1980 that profoundly influenced my life and shaped my theological explorations. This book is written in gratitude for that connection, which was made so many years ago yet continues to open the way ahead.

When I was a young adult, life had not gone as I expected. My walk of faith did not produce the quality of life that I wanted. There was a gap between how I was taught to practice faith, the results I thought I could anticipate, and the actual results my faith yielded. My heart knew a gospel my head could not practice. To put it plainly this was difficult to bear. It was crushing at times, and I struggled to make sense of and stay engaged with myself, others, and God.

Before I entered Princeton Theological Seminary in 1975, I began to study the theology of Jürgen Moltmann and found his work to be difficult but incredibly engaging. There was something different that aroused my attention about the way Moltmann's theological reflections engaged Scripture. His way was direct and surprisingly candid. In his insights I could hear recognition of the gap I had experienced and a fresh approach to filling it. In his dense and increasingly copious theology, I began to find a different kind of hope, a different kind of life addressing me and

1

offering me a new way to encounter God. Why had I never heard the "good news" presented in such a way before and why weren't more people talking about this man's work?

An unexpected opportunity to dig deeper into his theology presented itself when Moltmann was invited to deliver the Warfield Lectures at Princeton Seminary in 1980. Even more exciting, my professor of biblical theology, Dr. J. Christiaan Beker, invited me to join him and Dr. Moltmann as his dinner guest. That night I gleaned what I could from their discussion, which began in English but often lapsed into German. Afterwards, Dr. Beker shared with me the trauma that Dr. Moltmann underwent as a young man during World War II. Dr. Beker, who himself suffered under the Nazis as a teenager, told me of Moltmann's experiences during the 1943 bombing of Hamburg and shared his assessment of the effect these experiences had on Dr. Moltmann's theology. While I could not fully grasp it at the time, I began to recognize that the hope to which Moltmann's theology pointed drew me over the gap that was dividing my life and put me on a whole new path. The traumas and failures that had caused my faith to fall to pieces were reconstructed over the next two decades by the hope Moltmann found at the heart of the gospel. Moltmann's hope spoke to my deepest despair and debilitating fear and awakened in me a sense of self that set me free.

Not until 2007, when Moltmann published a "short theological biography" in his book *Experiences of God* did I fully realize why his theology affected me so deeply. Writing what he called a "theological biography" Moltmann confirmed that he had always viewed his theology as both a scholastic and a personal endeavor. He describes his work as "a fascinating adventure, though a dangerous one too." As he asks life's hardest questions, borne out of his own fear and despair, he acknowledges, "One can only stand up to it by exerting all one's heart and all one's soul and all one's strength."[1] It was indeed gratifying to learn that the questions I had been asking about this

---

1. Moltmann, *Experiences of God*, 9.

life of faith were the same questions he had been asking and answering all along.

Moltmann's theology has taught me that the very existence of hope itself is evidence of God's life dwelling within and around the people of God's creation. His insights have become central to my work as a pastor and to my journey of hope, leading me to read his theology on two tracks; one to discover theological insights, the other to discern how Moltmann himself received God's life-giving power and how this power can be lived out. Over the years I have discovered that with every new volume of theology, Moltmann uncovers a deeper expression of the life-giving hope of God's love. New theological insights emerged as Moltmann discovered how God's hope transformed the life of faith and revealed God's future in the world. His writings reveal a journey in which hope rose up in him as he was indwelt by God's empathy, held within the community of the suffering, drawn forward into foretastes of the new creation and finally, participated in sharing traces of the "full-filled life" with others.

The theology of Jürgen Moltmann and the stories in this book help me make sense out of life as it is linked to the life of God. My stories illustrate the central insights of Moltmann's theology and narrate what is fundamental to his work; that God dwells in every person as an inward guide, and that God encompasses everyone and everything. The stories illustrate how by dwelling in and encompassing all things, God is drawing all things into his own future.[2]

I am now convinced that every time a hopeful story is told, God is the unseen storyteller, "whispering" his empathy, encouragement, and guidance for life. Within every person God is welling up with hope in the midst of hopelessness. As God speaks in and through people's stories, God's immanence awakens the image of God in every person, showing forth every person's purpose in this world and calling each one into a relationship with God. Through this relationship people find hope in God's life within them.

2. Moltmann, *Theology of Hope*, 17; Moltmann, *Experiences of God*, 31.

I am further convinced that every person's story is a hopeful story waiting to be told. God's life encompasses everyone as an embrace of hopeful love, beckoning every person to allow his or her story to become a part of God's hopeful story. God makes room for every person's story to be included in his own story, beginning with the most sorrowful, distressing and tragic. Held in the transcendence of God, people sense that "in everything God is waiting for them,"[3] waiting to share with them the fulfillment of his life.

I am convinced that God's embrace of love indwells and encompasses every person and gathers their stories into his story, uniting the willing into one destiny. God's embrace beckons every person to be drawn into a metanarrative of God's creative resolve to fulfill his promises. God's activity rescues people from the shadow of death, draws them into a fellowship of love and destines them to share in the new creation of all things.

I tell stories to share the hope that now rises in me with great anticipation of what will one day be abundantly complete. As I share these stories, I invite you to hear God whispering words of hope into your life and to find your place within God's larger story. I encourage you to identify parts of your life with portions of the stories and then perceive how you are being beckoned and what such beckoning evokes in you. While the settings, characters, plots, and outcomes are simply aspects of my own and others' lives; they hold the potential to address the suffering and hope that is part and parcel of all our lives. Moltmann's theology has proven true in my own life and I believe will show its truth in yours as well. It is my hope that my stories engender your participation in God's work of bringing hope and life out of suffering and death—yours, others and mine. There is no doubt that Moltmann's theology is difficult. Even so, glean what you can from the theological sections of each chapter and let the stories draw you into the life God is seeking to share with each and every one of us . . . you, Moltmann, and me.

3. Moltmann, *Spirit of Life*, 36.

1

Hope for the Journey

(Eschatological Hope)

Hidden within every person's story,
the love story of the God of hope is being told.[1]

D ENNIS RAINEY TELLS THE story of a family vacation one
summer on a lake in northern Minnesota. One afternoon
the father was in the boathouse as his five-year-old son, Billy,
wandered down by the lake and out onto the dock. Seeing a
shiny metal canoe tied up to the dock, Billy attempted to
get into the boat, but lost his footing and fell into the lake.
Fortunately his father heard the splash and came running out
onto the dock. Not seeing his son on the surface of the water he
dove into the lake but could not find him. After surfacing for
air he again dove to search the dark waters, finding nothing.
Surfacing a second time, he took a deep breath and dove back
into the murky water. Deep under the water he finally spotted
Billy clinging tightly to one of the wooden piers. Swimming
over to him he pried his son's fingers off the pier, took hold of
him and raised him to the surface where he and Billy were able

1. Moltmann, *Trinity and the Kingdom*, 157.

5

to take a deep breath of air. Once on the shore the two of them rested and after a while the father asked his son, "Billy, what were you doing down there?" His son replied, "Just waiting for you Daddy, just waiting for you."[2]

Billy's story moves me to hope that parents can rescue every son and daughter trapped in perilous circumstances. We can also hear the story from Billy's perspective, lost in the darkness of the murky water yet willing to venture the hope that his father would soon appear to embrace him and save his life. Witnessing this little boy's trust in his father's care, I cannot help but notice that while under water Billy did not take account of his own hopefulness and assess his ability to rescue himself. No, Billy knew nothing but to entrust himself to hope and wait. He waited and entrusted his future to his father's care.

Stories like Billy's are analogies of every person's struggle for life in the midst of suffering and death.[3] They become a part of God's "supreme analogy"[4] in which those who are trapped by the inevitability of death are given tastes of a new quality of life that foretells the new creation of all things. These foretastes of new life instill a living hope in us, which gives us confidence to trust God in the midst of suffering and the entrapment of death.

Hope is a difficult commodity to muster in times of desperation and despair. When we find ourselves metaphorically buried under eight feet of water, we often have to look for a source of hope outside ourselves. If, like Billy, we are able to hang on and wait, the story we begin to hear narrated within us points to the fulfillment of a promise given outside ourselves.[5] As we recognize the analogous parts of our story and the greater story of God's coming kingdom, we begin to find our place in the story of salvation. Yet the actual rescue is fictional until we discover that the Rescuer is dwelling in our own desperation, and yes, in the desperation of *all* those who are held down and

---

2. Manning, *Ruthless Trust*, 95 (adaptation of story).

3. Moltmann, *God in Creation*, 61.

4. Ibid., 71.

5. Ibid., 63.

back in this world.[6] This "power in weakness" is its own witness and produces anticipation of what could be, instilling hope and eventually trust in a future fulfillment.

But what if Billy's story had ended before his father came to the rescue? I cannot help but wonder how a story like Billy's must torture parents who haven't been able to rescue their children. A similar emptiness comes over me every time I read Moltmann's account of "Operation Gomorrah," the planned destruction of Hamburg and the death of his school friend, Gerhard Schopper who was blown "to pieces" next to him during the bombing.[7] The finality of death is an overwhelming emptiness and we have all seen this finality rob the living of vitality. Nevertheless, out of this vast emptiness, the power of hope mysteriously drew Moltmann and "provided the strength to get up again after every inward and outward defeat."[8] This profound experience of hope in the midst of death is precisely what motivated Moltmann to write a theology of hope, explaining the presence and trajectory of hope in our lives. For over sixty-five years, he has taken the opportunity to journey with others on this path, beckoned together by the experience of a new creation dawning on their shared horizon.

Moltmann's story is a witness that in times of desperation, a strength not our own encompasses hopelessness and a wisdom from beyond us introduces our imaginations to a provisional design of what can be.[9] The appearance of hope into the darkness of despair pulls us into its embrace like the arms of a father rescuing his child, freeing the child from all that holds them down. Hope draws us into its expansive embrace, makes room for us, and begins to set us free from all that seeks our demise. As we submit to this embrace we are submitting ourselves into the divine nature of hope.

6. Moltmann, *Crucified God*, 249.

7. Moltmann, *In the End—the Beginning*, 33.

8. Moltmann, *Experiences of God*, 8.

9. Moltmann, *God in Creation*, 62.

The stories of the Bible tell us that the embrace of the God of hope rescues us all. The story of Billy's rescue portrays our vulnerability to hopelessness and death and God's willingness to dive into the darkness with us in order to pull us out. It depicts God coming into the world in the Son, taking hold of people, making them his own and then transporting them by the power of the Holy Spirit out of the realm of darkness and death and into God's life. The story of Billy's rescue reminds us of the depth of God's love for all people. Like Billy's father, God comes around us, transporting us to safety with his embrace of love.[10]

According to Moltmann, the Bible reveals that God sent the Son into the world to enter into human suffering and death so that in dying he might "once for all" take into himself the God-forsakenness of human life and death. Moltmann recognizes that by employing God's "unconquerable power of love," the Son took hold of people and, bearing them in himself, "emptied" himself into death.[11] Through this surrender Christ rescued us from the power of sin, hopelessness and death.[12] Simultaneously, as the Spirit employed this same unconquerable power to raise the Son out of death, the power of death was broken.[13] As the risen Son pours out the Spirit on all people, everyone is given the opportunity to be rescued from death and to participate in the new creation of all things.

Moltmann recognizes that the initial rescue of hope provides believers with "a confident hope" that what has begun in the present will be fulfilled in the future.[14] Reflection on this hope in Moltmann's writings has inspired me to tell stories from my own life where hope embraces fear and suffering, begins to transform them and unites us with the life of God. Stories like Billy's rescue have opened my eyes to hope, provid-

10. Moltmann, *Spirit of Life*, 278–79.

11. Moltmann, *Sun of Righteousness, Arise!*, 93.

12. Moltmann, *Coming of God*, 230–31; Moltmann, *Crucified God*, 249.

13. Moltmann, *Coming of God*, 232.

14. Moltmann, *Theology of Hope*, 228–29.

ing momentary glimpses of the believer's union with God. Such stories narrate what theologians call eschatological hope, a taste of what will one day fully be. Moltmann's theology explains the foundations for hope, providing examples of just exactly how God releases this hope out into the world.

In reflecting on his purpose for so thoroughly compiling a theology of hope, Motmann writes, "My whole concern has been, and still is to stimulate other people to discover theology for themselves—to have their own theological ideas, and to set out along their paths."[15] This celebrated theologian values his theological explorations as they inspire others to discover their own understanding of God as the source of hope. Out of death, ever-new life springs forth, and God indwells hope in the lives all those he loves.[16] None shall be excluded from tasting the hope of the new creation that God is bringing into the world.

And so the story telling has begun. Through these stories be beckoned by hope, drawn by love and transformed by the life of the triune God. May the narration of hope come alive in your own story.

---

15. Moltmann, *Experiences in Theology*, xv.
16. Moltmann, *Sun of Righteousness, Arise!*, 152.

2

Letting It Come to Us
(Immanence & Transcendence)

THE BEST BLESSINGS IN life are often unexpected. They have a way of finding us. They come to us, delight us and inspire us, drawing us beyond the boundary of the expected and endowing a goodness upon us that exceeds our explanation. So often as we look back over the decades, the things for which we are most grateful have little to do with our own achievements. Each of them has come as a gift.

Some years ago, the Buchanan family was given just such a gift on a family vacation to the Big Island of Hawaii. While all of the Hawaiian Islands are gifts of beauty, the beauty of the Big Island is found in its contrasts. Green shorelines stunningly outlined by black lava rock introduce visitors to rainforests, waterfalls, lava-spewing volcanoes, and two 10,000-foot peaks. Even amidst this magnificence, our family quickly realized that not all the island's beauty was found above water. While snorkeling together, we fell in love with a world that lies just beneath the surface, full of beautiful coral, spectacular rock formations, and brightly colored tropical fish. As we enjoyed this underwater world, we had no idea that the momentary joy of snorkeling would gift us with a blessing that remains even today.

Early one morning as we were about to slip into the water, a school of medium sized dolphins began surfacing about fifty yards off shore. The dolphins were swimming so fast that as they jumped into the air many of them were coming completely out of the water. I was amazed at what we were seeing and something stirred deep within me. What looked like a joyful celebration of life was drawing me toward it. Could my seven-year-old son and I venture out to swim with the dolphins? He and I had become good snorkeling partners. We had developed a routine where I did the swimming and he held the waistband of my swimsuit while floating alongside and snapping photos with his underwater camera. After consulting with my wife, my son and I decided to venture out together.

Everything seemed fine until we came to the edge of the shoreline shelf. As I continued to swim ahead, I noticed that we were no longer just ten to fifteen feet above the ocean floor. We were swimming into the darkness of deep water. After taking several more strokes, the white sand of the beach completely disappeared, and I felt myself suddenly giving into fear. I had to work to keep my composure. Reminding myself of what I had seen from the shoreline, I kept telling myself, "Keep pulling. Just keep pulling. This is your opportunity to experience something very special."

I pushed through my trepidation, and just as I was beginning to adjust to my surroundings, something moved far below us. The massive size of a shadowy figure sent waves of fear racing through me. As I realized how defenseless we were, I suddenly regretted putting my son and myself in such danger. I stopped swimming to get a better look at the ominous threat that we were facing. Before I could do anything else, another large figure appeared and then another. The longer I looked the more figures appeared. To my great surprise, I could now see that the large figures were swimming in formation. Relief flooded over me. My dread turned to awe as I realized we were in the presence of a pod of very large dolphins. These were not the dolphins we had seen from the shore. These were Bottlenose Dolphins, six or seven feet in length and nine hundred to a thousand pounds in weight. As I stared in amazement, I recognized that this pod of wild animals was rising up underneath us.

I collected myself and began swimming again and realized several baby dolphins were in the pod, swimming in perfect alignment with their mothers. In the silence it felt as though the dolphins were strangely aware of our presence. For a moment I imagined what Zach and I looked like to them, swimming side by side like a mother and baby dolphin. As I continued swimming I felt beckoned into their gentle rhythm and into the safety of their number. They continued to rise up beneath us, and a surprising calm came over me. I felt myself drawn into their serenity. Again I stopped swimming, but this time not in fear, rather in surrender to the beauty and peace of the dolphins' presence.

Mesmerized by the tranquil pod, which rose up beneath us, we were unaware that an even more intimate encounter awaited us. Following close behind the mothers and their babies, a group of larger dolphins drew up to not more than a few yards below us. As if to acknowledge our presence, the lead dolphin rose up and slowly turned right in front of us. As he turned the whole formation followed behind him, surfacing, turning and passing stunningly close to us.

There we were, surrounded by Bottlenose Dolphins encircling us with their massive bodies, majestically streaming by us. We were captivated by the royal parade of strength, dignity and discipline. The encounter transported me away from every earthly concern and for a moment, I lost track of time and space. I felt at one with all that surrounded me. Only the click, click, click of my son's camera brought me back into the present moment. Realizing the opportunity before me, I reached out my hand to try touching what was just beyond my reach. Spiritually, the passing of this pod of dolphins gifted us with a sense of serenity we had never experienced before. Faced with an amazing display of power, cooperation and coordination, I felt a oneness with life that I could never experience on my own.

It felt as if we had been chosen that day to taste the dolphin's harmony with one another just under the surface of the water.

That night as we recalled our dolphin encounter, our remembrances included not only what we had seen and sensed that day but our emotional and spiritual responses as well. The experience spoke deeply to each of us. Journeying out beyond the familiar and into deep water, we were drawn past our fears and into a wondrous connection with beings so unlike ourselves. For us it was an extraordinary experience that convinced us we had been addressed from beyond. Through our participation in the unexpected, a taste of life and peace rose up around us and shared itself with us. In the dolphins' response to us, we experienced the extraordinary nature of God's life and peace. The life of God that we sensed through nature drew us up into an assurance that it has not been overcome by the powers of death and disorder. Just a taste witnessed to us that God has the power to embrace people's lives and to share with them the quality of God's own life and peace.

This extraordinary embrace became a metaphor for the life of faith. As we swam out beyond the safety of the shoreline shelf and into the darkness of unknown waters, we learned that God could be trusted out in the deep darkness of life in this world. Then and now God surprises us with hope, beauty, peace and the reality of being found and known when we can no longer protect ourselves or secure life's beauty for ourselves. In the dark waters of the Pacific, where we ourselves were powerless, God's love embraced us and we felt indwelt by the harmony and peace of God's own life. What we were taught was the wisdom of God: that being found, known and indwelt are prerequisites to finding, knowing and indwelling God. As we are found, known and indwelt we taste a way of life beyond what our own abilities can create or sustain.

As a family we are convinced that this surprising encounter with dolphins and the internal blessings that grew out of it did not take place because we were good swimmers or because we exercised extraordinary faith. The indwelling of God's presence in the peace and solemnity of the dolphins was shared with us as a sacred gift. After my son and I returned to shore, we told my wife, Susan, all about our encounter. Inspired by our wonder and joy, she swam out on her own, overcoming her fear of swimming out over the ledge into the dark and bottomless ocean. There she, too, encountered the dolphins and enjoyed her own experience of the majestic creatures swimming under and around her. In retelling the story from her experience, Susan always exclaims, "And I hardly know how to swim!" Susan's awareness of her own limited ability explains how and why encountering the dolphins was holy and hopeful. She now looks to find the holy in every aspect of her life. Beginning with the dolphin encounter, Susan is learning to trust what Jesus proclaimed, "My Father is still working and I also am working" (John 5:17). The holy is at work in all things.

The process by which God made himself known to us in the encounter of the dolphins mirrored Jürgen Moltmann's process of recognizing God's activity in the world and his theological description of it. Just as our physical encounter with the dolphins led us to an awareness of God's intangible activity, so Moltmann begins his theological reasoning by reflecting upon tangible experiences of life that point to "the effects" of God's intangible activity in people's personal and collective stories.[1] Hope is the first "effect" of God's activities that believers may discern both in the mundane and the extraordinary, in times of distress and exhilaration.

Moltmann maintains that every person has the opportunity to discern the hope of God's activity within their experience (God's immanence) and their experience within the life of God (God's transcendence).[2] He calls this "learning"[3] for while God makes this hope available, it must be perceived, accepted, and "learned." This "learned hope" represents a profound expansion of the Christian's experience of God. It is not learning

1. Moltmann, *Coming of God*, xvi.
2. Moltmann, *Spirit of Life*, 7, 35.
3. Moltmann, *Experiences of God*, 19.

about the believer's activity of faith, or about God's activity of indwelling; rather it is perceiving, accepting, and experiencing God's activity. As we experience hope we discover that it is not something we take possession of, it is something that takes possession of us.

Moltmann identifies this divine activity as the first effect (or fruit) of God's "mutual indwelling." This "mutual indwelling" is God's investment of himself, which penetrates and dwells in another for the other's benefit. I describe this activity as God's embrace of human flesh. Stated simply God's mutual indwelling is God's love in action within and among people. As God indwells us, we are beckoned to receive the benefit of his embrace of hopefulness and love in and around us. This hopefulness beckons us to be hopeful, filled with expectation and then to participate in God's indwelling by sharing it with others.

Such learning and sharing initiates the wondrous way of being, yet it occurs not apart from life lived in this world but *in the midst of* living. It does not take place at our own initiative or as an act of our will. We learn hope as we experience it apart from our own resolve and strength. We learn hope as Moltmann has written, "in the experiences life brings us."[4] We learn hope as we are tested and there God's hope finds us.

Moltmann confirms that this method "grew up" out of experiences of his own life. He writes, "The road emerged as I walked it. And my attempts to walk it are of course determined by my personal biography."[5] It was for Moltmann a "tremendous adventure . . . into the unknown with many surprises."[6] Certainly his greatest surprise was that hope rose as a gift out of Christ's suffering, dying and rising. In the hopelessness of Moltmann's own suffering, remorse, and loss, God's hope broke through and identified itself. This hope opened his eyes to the possibility of a God who could accompany, companion, and

---

4. Ibid.
5. Moltmann, *Experiences in Theology*, xv.
6. Moltmann, *Coming of God*, xiv.

love him. As he writes, "I cannot even say I found God . . . But I do know in my heart . . . that he found me."[7]

In every person's life experience, the God of hope waits. God indwells the full array of human experience, waiting to indwell and encompass every person's experience with hope. For my family in Hawaii God's hope indwelt our vulnerability, fear, and eventual exhilaration. For Moltmann God's hope indwelt his suffering, remorse, and despair. Moltmann argues that the very existence of hope is evidence of God rising up with love to unite all things with himself. Just the prospect of such a union allows hope to rise where it is least expected, out of life's greatest disappointments, debilitating losses, destructive acts of violence, and injustice.

Moltmann's life's story is a poignant illustration of this. A victim of the World War II bombing of Hamburg, Germany, Moltmann suffered the loss of his friend and fellow anti-aircraft gunner as the teenagers defended their home city. Traumatized by the horrific death of his friend as well as other deaths he witnessed while serving on the front lines, Moltmann descended into isolation and despair when he was taken as a prisoner of war. In his years of imprisonment Moltmann could not rise to meet God. He writes, "In the first year particularly it was for me a struggle with the question about God. Like Jacob, wrestling at the brook of Jabbok with a dark and mysterious angel, I tormented myself with God's dark and mysterious side, with his hidden face and his deadly 'no' which had put me in misery behind barbed wire."[8] Yet after reading the book of Psalms and the Gospel of Mark while imprisoned, Moltmann began to perceive that God's hidden face had always been empathetically turned toward him and others in the camp. Slowly, he began to experience "the light of his countenance."

Through Christ's suffering as depicted in the gospel of Mark, Moltmann recognized himself to be embraced by God. He writes that when he heard Jesus' death cry, "I knew with

7. Moltmann, *Experiences of God*, 9.
8. Moltmann, *In the End—the Beginning*, 9.

certainty: this is someone who understands you. I began to understand the assailed Christ because I felt that he understood me: this was the divine brother in distress who takes the prisoners with him on his way to resurrection."[9] Moltmann not only identified with Christ's forsakenness, but also found his own suffering and sense of desolation "held up from afar."[10] Moltmann perceived that he was "taken with" Christ and Christ companioning him as he faced his despair as well as the remorse he and his countrymen bore over their complicity in the atrocities committed against the Jews. In this companionship Moltmann recognized the suffering Jesus to be the Son of God. Through the Son's empathy Moltmann experienced himself being gathered up and united with the Son's suffering, crucifixion, and resurrection. Through this experience he tasted for the first time the hope of the resurrection deep within himself. Moltmann describes these early experiences of hope as a time when "my senses awoke and I could love life again. For me that was an hour of liberation. I could breathe freely again and felt like a human being once more."[11]

For Moltmann the awakening of hope did not come "all of sudden or overnight" but from being beckoned and drawn over a period of months and years. He writes about his experiences as a prisoner of war. "How often I walked round and round in circles at night in front of the barbed wire fence. My first thoughts were always about the free world outside, from which I was cut off, but I always ended up thinking about a centre to the circle in the middle of the camp—a little hill, with a hut on it, which served as a chapel. It seemed to me like a circle surrounding the mystery of God, which was drawing me towards it."[12] Out of the indwelling love of God, hope was born. The new birth of hope brought with it what he describes as re-creation, a time when the *imago dei*, the image of God, was

9. Moltmann, *Source of Life*, 5.

10. Moltmann, *Experiences of God*, 8.

11. Moltmann, *Broad Place*, 34–35.

12. Moltmann, *Experiences of God*, 8.

restored. As Moltmann encircled the camp, a new identity was being conceived in him, the identity of those held in the crucified and risen Christ, the *imago Christi* or image of Christ.[13] Just as awe mysteriously raised my son and I up into the union of creation and Creator so in the midst of Moltmann's despair the Son's suffering released him from his alienation and united him with the love of the suffering God.

The story of a prisoner of war walking the perimeter of his captivity and the story of a father and son being encircled by dolphins in the depths of the Pacific provide images of the immanent and transcendent presence of God in human life. Moltmann's experience of circling, of being drawn into the Son whose suffering bore both his own and the world's suffering, gave birth to hope within him. This hope within provides an image of the *immanent* embrace of God in human life. The circling of the dolphins beneath and around us portrayed for us the adventure of being raised up into the *transcendent* embrace of God of human life. Wondrously when God both indwells human life (the immanence of God) and human life is held in God (the transcendence of God) the new creation of all things begins. When the two provisionally intersect they "interpenetrate each other mutually."[14] When this occurs, the creative powers of God are released, at first birthing hope, then a new identity, and then a new sharing of divine and human life. The theological term for this creative work is God's immanent transcendence.[15] When we perceive God's Spirit rising up, encircling us, sharing with us the power of God's love, we are made a part of God's story and the new creation begins.

The implications of this are profound. The Christian faith is never about us making ourselves, our actions, our lives good enough for God. It is about being drawn into the divine life. It is about the three persons of God sharing themselves with us in distinctive ways that draw us into their own reciprocal sharing

13. Moltmann, *God in Creation*, 226.

14. Moltmann, *Sun of Righteousness, Arise!*, 169

15. Moltmann, *Spirit of Life*, 34–35; Moltmann, *Coming of God*, 73.

of life and love. The bold truth is that none of us apprehend for ourselves or receive the gifts of God's presence because we warrant them. No, we are drawn into the way of life the New Testament writers call grace (Eph 2:4–10). While the practice of "letting it come to us" is a learned discipline, it is the means by which an authentic encounter of the triune God takes place. It finds us.[16] Surely, letting it come to us is the way of living which leads to the one thing we cannot provide ourselves, life.[17] This fundamental affirmation is one of Jürgen Moltmann's greatest contributions to theological thought.

Hope beckons us to encounter God in the deep waters of our lives where fear and vulnerability, suffering and death reside. Drawn by hope we are beckoned to cup our hands, to flutter kick our feet and as cautiously as we choose, to take one stroke after another as we pass into the deep waters where God has chosen to rise up around us and in us with his own life. If we had stayed where we could see the bottom, falsely believing we had some control, we would have never known the blessing of God's own life coming into our fleeting lives. Without venturing into the deep waters of life and death we might have learned how to keep our head above water close to shore, but we would have never been drawn into the waters where God chooses to come to us, rising up underneath us and encompassing us with the hope of new life.

---

16. Moltmann, *Spirit of Life*, 21, 27, 127.
17. Moltmann, *Sun of Righteousness, Arise!*, 162.

3

A Plan to Prosper, Not to Harm
(Adoption in the Son)

IN 1986 I TRAVELED to Salvador, Brazil, to meet my eight-month-old son for the first time. On that day, I found myself filled with both great anticipation and great anxiety. While I was focused on all the logistical matters of the adoption process, I was also cognizant that what was about to take place would profoundly alter this child's destiny as well as my own. I sensed myself being swept forward toward what I could only hope would be an auspicious moment in both of our lives.

Deep within me I wondered, were all the promises that I firmly believed had led me to this day going to be kept? Was the custody I was about to assume the initiation of a destiny that would be fulfilling for this little boy? Would he sense in my touch the capacity to contain his anxiety and calm his fears about the future? Would he find in my embrace a sense of hopefulness and peace? These questions drove me to pray, "Is there something more than just my own desire to adopt that has led me to this child and this child to me? Take hold of what we begin this day and make it your own, Lord." While the short prayer calmed my nerves, it did little to answer my questions and dissolve my apprehension.

After a brief taxi ride, I met the social worker that had arranged the adoption. Together we walked a short distance to a designated café. It was a sunny morning, yet the humid tropical air soaked up the brightness of the sun. As if to announce that this was indeed a special day, everything that morning was surrounded by a soft glow of light. While we walked I questioned my perception of what was quickly becoming surreal. The colors around me seemed more vivid than usual, and people seemed to be wearing halos that shimmered with light. As I looked ahead, I saw a small figure propped up on a vendor's stand sitting like a Buddha statue for all to see. I don't know whether it was my own anxiety or the glow of light in the air, but I struggled to get a fix on his plump little body. As I drew closer all I could see was his brown skin and his dark curly hair glistening in the sunlight. Then in a single moment I was able to distinguish his face from his body and our eyes met.

Time both expanded and shrank in that instant. Before I could look deeply into his eyes and see all that was hidden there, his eyes sparkled with excitement and joy, and an ever widening smile broke out on his face. It was a sparkle and a smile I will never forget. I was delighted to receive such a joyful greeting. I wondered then and still wonder today if the delight on his face was simply a reflection of what was shining on my face or a reflection of a more significant Presence which began to illuminate the pathway of our new destiny together.

What I have learned as the parent of an adopted child is that the custody you assume covers every aspect of the child's life, not just the child's physical well-being. It includes custody of the child's emotional and spiritual development as well. Everything that brings life to a son or daughter is placed in your hands. This includes the oversight of a very complex process of melding the child's old identity as an orphan with their new identity as your adopted son or daughter. This is an arduous process for most adopted children, for hidden within their memory is the experience of being abandoned. Adoptive parents—innocently unaware of the sorrow this memory evokes—are at a loss for how to help the child receive their new destiny and live into the opportunity of being part of a new family.

Regrettably, the memory of abandonment imprints shame upon the orphan's internal self-concept. Many feel both forsaken and "forsake-able." They perceive themselves to be unworthy of a parent's love and care. Untethered from the source of their life, they fear the future and cannot rid themselves of the perception that they are destined for a life of neglect and deprivation. The fear of abandonment is never far away.

What I now know more than twenty-five years later is that the adopted child's greatest need is to be affirmed as he or she is. Physical hugs provide the child a tangible experience of safety and of welcome. Words that affirm the child's value and express delight in his or her presence assure the child of belonging. Yet the most important embrace is not seen or heard but is intangibly detected in the parent's devotion to the child. Without this clear devotion, the child continues to struggle with insecurity and a fear of the future. Providing the child guidance and discipline in a structured environment is important, yet it is the embrace of unconditional love over time which holds the power to free the adopted child from the past. This unconditional love establishes a relationship able to endure disappointments and misunderstandings and to remain strong even in the midst of broken promises real or perceived.

The reality is that every parent/child relationship and every person's future is bound by time and fleeting in nature. Like adopted children every one of us desires the assurance that our future is secure under parental care. Some have unjustly been excluded from knowing such a destiny exists. Others have experienced themselves being beckoned into it but have chosen to turn their backs on all that God offers. Even for those who know and believe, none of us can assure ourselves of our own inclusion. We all are dependent upon expressions of love and care from outside ourselves to communicate to us the assurances we need. Such a testimony is provided by the inward whispers of

God's Spirit and by the outward testimony of the "great cloud of witnesses," the adopted children of God.

This assurance is given when in recognition of the adopting Father's presence, the Spirit cries out within the child, "Abba, Father" (Rom 8:15–16). In that moment we experience the eternal Father as a power so personal and so accessible that something within us cries out, "Papa, you are here!" Such a realization fills the empty places in "the parentless child's" inward self and provides a new identity as God's own child. When we experience such recognition, we receive what the Apostle Paul calls "the spirit of adoption," the spirit of the Father's presence wholly embracing us (Rom 8:15). It is this spirit that enables each of us to boldly declare to others, "See what love the Father has given us, that we should be called children of God; and that is what we are" (1 John 3:1). The indwelling of God's Spirit enables the children of God to believe in and testify to one another about their new destiny of life.

According to Jürgen Moltmann, this new destiny was initiated in the event of the cross of Christ. It was then unveiled in the raising of the one who was crucified as the Son of God who eternally lives to bring life out of death for all who will receive it.[1] Moltmann recognizes that in choosing to give his only Son over to death, God was exchanging God's destiny of eternal life for the human destiny of death. He writes, "God overcomes sin and the death of his creatures by taking their destiny on himself . . . by entering into the God-forsakenness of sin and death . . . God overcomes it and makes it part of his eternal life."[2] As was written to the church at Ephesus, "He [God] destined us for adoption as his children through Jesus Christ according to the good pleasure of his will . . . In Christ we have also obtained an inheritance, having been destined according to the purpose of him who accomplishes all things according to his counsel and will, so that we, who were the first to set our hope in Christ, might live for the praise of his glory" (Eph 1:5, 11–12).

---

1. Moltmann, *Crucified God*, 244–45.
2. Moltmann, *God in Creation*, 90–91.

Moltmann declares that such a wondrous exchange "destines men and women to the image of God"[3] and provides them a place in the family of God. Through the work of the Spirit, adopted children receive both an outward and inward confirmation of God's wondrous activity. With their ears they hear fellow family members giving God praise and thanks for the love that reconciles them to God and to each other. Inwardly the Spirit awakens God's image, placed in every person at creation to confirm their identity as God's own children and enlivens an inner love that creates family and makes room for new members. Adopted children begin to bear, in their relationship with one another and God, an ability to stay connected while retaining their individual identity. Moltmann understands this to be a new "sociality" which is reflective of God's ability to extend and receive a mutuality of love and care.[4]

Moltmann's experience of being found by God in his "dark night of the soul" witnesses to "the spirit of adoption" exchanging a destiny of death for a destiny of life. He experienced God adopting those who were suffering enabling them to find new life in the love of God and the family of God. As a prisoner of war during World War II, Moltmann found companionship in the suffering Son of God. While in confinement he read of Jesus' crucifixion with new eyes. Moltmann writes in his autobiography, "Jesus' God-forsakenness on the cross showed me where God is present—where he was in my experiences of death, and where he is going to be in whatever comes."[5] He understood that the very experiences that rendered him helpless before death's destructive power and hopeless before his own life were precisely where God was present and is to be found. While such companionship in suffering caught his attention, fulfilled hope remained out of reach until he experienced God's assurance through human forgiveness. His new brothers and sisters in the family of God ministered much-needed acceptance to

3. Moltmann, *Trinity and the Kingdom*, 118.

4. Moltmann, *Spirit of Life*, 94, 219.

5. Moltmann, *Broad Place*, 31.

him. Moltmann testifies, "For me the turn from humiliation to new hope came about through two things—first through the Bible and then through the encounter with other people."[6] In his autobiography he shares how powerfully he was affected by the kindness of strangers as well as the words and actions of other Christians. Moltmann describes the unexpected mercies he received as a POW:

> The kindness with which Scots and English, our former enemies, came to meet us half way . . . the miners and their families took us in with a hospitality that shamed us profoundly. We heard no reproaches; we were accused of no guilt. We were accepted as people, even though we were just numbers and wore our prisoners' patches on our backs. We experienced forgiveness of guilt without a confession of guilt on our part, and that made it possible for us to live with the past of our people, and in the shadow of Auschwitz, without repressing anything and without becoming callous.[7]

Later, Moltmann recounts:

> The other experience [which] turned my life upside down was the first international Student Christian Movement conference at Swanwick, in the summer of 1947, to which a group of POWs was invited . . . And we came with fear and trembling. What were we to say about the war crimes, and the mass murders in the concentration camps? But we were welcomed as brothers in Christ, and were able to eat and drink, pray and sing with young Christians who had come from all over the world. In the night my eyes sometimes filled with tears.[8]

Coupled with a newfound connection to God, this testimony of kindness, welcome, and shared worship revealed to Moltmann that there is indeed consolation amidst loss, that the

6. Moltmann, *Source of Life*, 4.
7. Moltmann, *Source of Life*, 5.
8. Ibid.

suffering and death of the Son bears all suffering and all death, and that God's devotion to bring his children life has never been broken. Even the dead of Auschwitz, in Hamburg and on both sides of the battlefront are not alone. Such devotion assures the abandoned that a new and wondrous future is coming. God as parent Father, Son and Holy Spirit is with, in and for all his children. What Paul says, Moltmann experienced. "We are children of God, and if children, then heirs, heirs of God and joint heirs with Christ—if, in fact, we suffer with him so that we may also be glorified with him" (Rom 8:16–17).

The new destiny into which God welcomes adopted children is already forged by the suffering love of God in the cross of Christ. Every adopted child walks the way of suffering love. Just as Christ holds each child's sadness, disappointments, and losses the adopted children of God are called to hold others' sadness, disappointments and losses. My own calling is to hold my adopted son's sadness and suffering in the embrace of God's unconditional love which creates for us a lifelong relationship. No difficulty, sorrowful misstep, or long period of separation can sever the relationship in which we are held. Our hope simply does not rest in ourselves.

About a year ago, my now adult son shared with me that he knows that "God has [his] back." He told me that in recovering from a difficult period in his life he discovered the goodness of God and that God was now seeing him through. With strength in his voice he said, "You are no longer my father. My Father is in heaven. He will take care of me." For a brief moment I was taken aback. Had I not suffered with my son? Did he not know my love? Yet the offense I felt was short lived. His Father was my Father as well. We both would know the destiny that the Heavenly Father provides. Deep within me a joy was dawning as I realized that the destiny I so wanted to provide that little boy I met in Brazil was now being enacted. My son was stepping into his new identity as a child of God. The embrace of God as his eternal Father was now drawing him ahead into an eternal blessing of belonging to the household of God. He has a home, a family and the Father to hold him and guide him forever.

My joy has multiplied as I have considered my son's new identity. Both of us have received the destiny of adoption in the embrace of the three persons of God and now we will forever have the same Father, living together as children of God. Such a shared identity resonates deeply within my own life. Broad indeed is the place where I reside with my adopted son. In this place there is no resentment, for our union is dependent not on our own doing but rather on the self-giving love of God, which we are discovering is an unending flow.

4

Face Down in the Ditch, Again
(Eternal Death)

B Y THE TIME I was in the third grade a lot had happened. I already carried the imprint of trauma suffered early in life. As a grade-schooler I knew that something wasn't right in me. I knew that I had gotten into more than my share of trouble yet I did not know why. I could not link what had occurred in the past with what I did in the present. While I did not like the label of "unmanageable" that adults assigned to me, I couldn't seem to shake it.

To put it mildly I was an energetic and enthusiastic kid. The problem was that I was energetic and enthusiastic about the wrong things at the wrong time. This made school both difficult for me and challenging for my teachers. As I grew older, I found myself increasingly dismayed about the difficulties I caused myself and increasingly remorseful about the problems I caused those I loved. While I longed to change, I felt powerless to do so.

In third grade I gained a sense of how easily things could spin out of control and I could find myself literally and figuratively lying face down in the ditch with nowhere to go. I had not listened to the new rules our teachers had devised and

announced earlier that week. Those of us who rode our bikes
to school now had regulated zones in which to park our bikes.
Unaware of these new rules, I parked (actually tossed) my bike
outside of the designated third grade zone. As a result, my bike
was confiscated, and I was told that in order to get my bike
back, I needed to address the principal and admit "my mis-
take." Looking out the office window at my bike, I refused to
acknowledge to the principal that the bike we were looking at
was mine and that I had parked it in a forbidden area. My refusal resulted in being told that I would be walking home after
school, and that my parents would be informed of all that had
taken place. Recognizing that, indeed, I would not have my bike
after school, I quickly devised a plan to recover it.

After lunch I slipped out of my classroom, ran to just outside the principal's office, stole my own bike, and rode it as fast
as I could past my third grade classrooms. As I frantically ped-
aled I looked up just in time to see my teacher looking squarely
at me as I rode by. Doomed and yet devoted to my plan I rode
directly to where I could hide my bike in some brush and ran
back to school to face my accusers. Nearing the school, I skin-
nied on my hands and knees up the dry ditch that ran next to
the playground. Lying there in the ditch, I realized that things
probably were not going to end well. I needed all the help I
could get, so I bowed my head and said my first prayer, "Dear
Jesus (I was Christo-centric then), please help me get out of this
trouble."

Yes, trouble was what I was in that day, and trouble like this
seemed to be a regular companion of mine from grade school
through high school and even as a young adult. As I grew older,
I began to realize how disruptive my impulsive behaviors were.
I recognized that no matter how hard I worked or how deeply
devoted I was, my occasional emotional outburst or impulsive
action tainted my relationships. While I did not know it at the
time, my failure to address the underlying problem left me destined to repeat unwanted patterns of behavior. Even as an adult,
bad things never seemed to get better and the damaging wake I

left behind continued to grow. Outwardly I remained energetic and enthusiastic but inwardly I was at loss to find a stable center that could guide me in times of stress and conflict. Struggling to access a new way of being, I continued to find myself face down in the proverbial ditch of my own making, locked down in a string of setbacks that I never wanted or anticipated.

Ashamed of my inability to manage my life, my erupting emotions, and my failing relationships, I had not granted Christ access to my inner self. While I gratefully received the grace of God that justified me as a sinner, I felt called to become more "Christlike" by committing myself to a lifetime journey of devotion and discipline. Yet no matter how ardently I tried, the Christ I loved was too pure, too holy for me. I could not find a place for the sin that clung to me so closely nor the chronic sense of unrest I felt. I was convinced that in the righteous presence of Christ there was no room for sin. A pervasive sense of isolation from God caused me to look again at my understanding of God's involvement in human life. At midlife, facing a divorce and what seemed like the end of the family and career I had worked so hard to piece together, I began searching for something that could overcome the rage that so unpredictably rose up and controlled me despite my best efforts to change.

The emotional wounds I carried from a single incident of physical abuse suffered as a seven-year-old boy had effectively robbed me of the governor of my internal engine. As a young boy I never questioned the judgment that unleashed such violent blows upon me. I just assumed that my wrongdoing was commensurate with the punishment I received, and that the judgment rendered was final. The angry punishment I received became the angry punishment I directed at myself. The rage inflicted on me became the rage I inflicted on others. Just like my third-grade self, hiding from my teacher, I kept these parts of my past out of sight, both hiding from and waiting for inevitable punishment. "My Jesus," as I understood him, had called me to be a better person before him, but had never allowed me to process my emotional woundedness with him, or to welcome him into my diminished self where the powers of destruction still seemed to reside.

On my thirty-seventh birthday, in the ditch yet again, I admitted to myself that my relationship with Christ did not provide me access to the regenerative powers of God. Divorced, living apart from my two adopted children, unsuccessfully looking to find a new call in ministry, I was rock bottom and forced to explore a new way of being in relationship with God, myself and others. Even when I believed that I approached the throne of grace with boldness, seeking grace to find help in my time of need, no such help was provided. I needed God's power to do more than just disentangle my failed aspirations and release me to make myself a better disciple of Christ. I needed God to remake my "sin full" inner core and to provide me a completely new "way of being" in and with him.

Forlorn at the prospect of a future with no power to set myself free from internal conflict and no resources to repel the darkness that was closing in on me, I fell into a debilitating depression. While I held a job as a carpenter, I could do little else. Each evening after work I sat alone motionless and without resolve for hours. Overcome by a sense of malaise, I faced the humiliating truth that I could do nothing about my own internal conflict and the despair it caused. I accepted my dependency and identified with the brokenhearted. As I let myself be known by God in all my vulnerability and shame, God did not turn away from me. Utterly dependent upon him, I noticed God's determination, his strength of will to include me in his life of love. I later identified this strength of will as God's resolve to include me in his own life. This inclusion provided me a new way of being in my own life and it gave me hope for a future that did not resemble the past. I wrote in my journal:

> Stuck down in my background,
> I have nowhere to go,
> Ground down in my background,
> I am knocked down and staying down,

> Struck down, shut down,
> locked down in a breakdown,
>
> There is a breakdown coming if I stay ground down.
> There is a new self coming round if my tears roll down,
> Backed down from my background,
> breaking ground not breaking down,
> Breaking ground, breaking free,
> breaking ground, finding me,
> There is a new self coming as my tears flow down.

As an increasingly vivid experience, I was embraced by a depth of divine empathy I had never experienced before. To my surprise even while despairing of life I was companioned. Within and around me I encountered an unexpected, "Yes, I am walking in your shame and your shameful self is walking in me." God's creative resolve forged a way to walk in and with my shame and sorrow. God made a new way forward by making his Son who knew no sin, "to be sin so that in him we might become the righteousness of God" (2 Cor 5:21). As the Son on the cross became sin for us, he walked the wayward path with me. To my great surprise, I was not alone in the shame and sorrow of my sin.

Jürgen Moltmann insightfully characterizes the death of the Son on the cross as "an eternal death" suffered for all people.[1] Moltmann explains, "By entering into the God forsakenness of sin and death, God can overcome it and make it part of his eternal life."[2] The Son has the eternal power of the Father to take custody over and bear in his death every person's waywardness, every act of violence and injustice, and even death itself. What I began to experience was that the waywardness of my own "sin full self" and the wrong that was done to me had been drawn into the Son who the Father had sent into the world to be sin for every person. I began to realize that the Son was

---

1. Moltmann, *Trinity and the Kingdom*, 80.
2. Moltmann, *God in Creation*, 91.

obedient to the Father in a way I had not been. His obedience eliminated my separation from the Father. Out of love for every person, the Son died to embrace everyone who will receive his death as the eternal death of sin and the end of separation from the Father. Through the Spirit's life-giving power, Christ was raised out of death, and through the outpouring of the Spirit, a new possibility has come into the world—Christ's new life can be shared with every person.

The grace of the triune God sharing life with those on the pathway of hope overwhelmed me then and overwhelms me even today. Embraced in this grace, every new moment holds the possibility of sharing life with God through Christ. This possibility was created by God's resolve to profoundly love all people and gather them into fellowship with him. It was this creative resolve that I encountered in the emptiness of my depression, and it gave me a vision of a future so broad and generous as to include me. Moltmann recognizes that the triune God "makes space" within himself even for the "forsakenness of sinners."[3]

Held in the space that God's resolve creates through the Son, I no longer belong to the offense of my sin and it does not belong to me. Old patterns of behavior learned during times of stress and in the midst of childhood conflicts have been emptied into Christ's death. The embrace of Christ's death sets me free to experience the living companionship of the three persons of God coming around and indwelling me as "the righteousness of God."

As I brought my shamed and hidden parts before God in prayer, I discovered that the Father, the Son, and the Holy Spirit are my companions who collectively rescued me from my earthly father's traumatizing judgment, my own self-condemnation and my own sin full response. The triune God was present through the Spirit to heal, restore, and grant me access through the Son to a new Father. Slowly I felt my shameful sorrow being embraced and my future set free from the past. As I

3. Moltmann, *Coming of God*, 298, 306–7.

witnessed God's full acceptance of all parts of me, I was placed on the path of self-acceptance and intimacy with God.

"How could this be?" I sometimes asked myself. If I was finally changing, how could I not be the one initiating and carrying out the changes? I had worked so hard before—why was change finally happening now? I sensed that whatever was taking place was a process occurring gradually within and around me. When I looked inward, I sensed that I was undergirded in a new way that gave me patience with myself. When I noticed what surrounded me, I felt drawn ahead into a new beginning. I sensed I was being set up on a new platform, a whole new place to be. Finally out of the all-too-familiar ditch and in a new place, I could see myself, my vulnerability, and my need for God. In this new place, there was space to perceive what God was doing in giving me a new identity and in introducing me to a new way of living in authentic community with God and others.

While I had tried for many years to force myself to change, Moltmann explains that the power of the cross is not found in its forcefulness or in its dominance but in the finality of its surrender. The Son "became poor" for the sake of humanity (2 Cor 8:9). The Son emptied himself on the cross so that every person might be given life through him (Phil 2:6–11). Because the Creator of all life surrendered to death the Son brings the possibility of ever new and everlasting life into every person's existence. As he died, that which the Son willingly bore within himself died with him. Just as Christ's power was in his surrender, my freedom began to arrive and still arrives in my own surrender. As I surrender, I continually find all that has separated me from people and from God is "swallowed up" in the death of the Son (1 Cor 15: 54–57). That which kept me trapped in a ditch died with Christ and lives no more.

In the embrace of the Son's "once for all" death, the past and the present are united as one, and together they are drawn forward into God's future. Moltmann calls this the "eschatological process"[4] of the cross. This process "pays backward and forward" while altering what is possible in the present. I have come to understand that Christ's death reached back into every facet of my life. It is the backward payment of the cross that initiated my new destiny and the forward payment that will someday complete it in full. It is the Son's payment into the present that creates ever new hope which inspires and empowers me (and every person) to live with trust in all that is to come through the Spirit, in the Son, and from the Father.

Just because I lived more than half of my life hiding and struck down, I no longer have to live as that person had "always been." In fact, nobody does. Moltmann recognizes that as the Son enters the world, the love of the triune God enters into both the loveless perpetrators and unloved victims of the world. He writes, "[God's love] can be crucified, but in crucifixion it finds its fulfillment and becomes love of the enemy." Through the Son's death, God's love "gives life even to its enemies and opens up the future to change."[5]

Putting our trust in the victory of the Son's eternal death frees us from destructive acts and awakens us to the power of love in every heart and every relationship, releasing us into the liberation and love of the triune God. This liberation, according to Moltmann, connects the freed with the powers of the new creation, which the love of the triune God is bringing into the world through the resurrection.

For me, the imprint of violence committed against me as a child ended in the death of the Son. While incrementally I experience myself freed from hiding facedown in the ditch, I live in the hope of a final release. My life, as Moltmann teaches, now "takes its definition from the future" the future of the Son, the Spirit, and the Father. What is now coming is the creative power of the Spirit to imprint within me and within all who belong to the Son, the attributes of Christ's self-giving love. Moltmann

---

4. Moltmann, *Crucified God*, 249.

5. Moltmann, *Crucified God*, 248–49.

calls it the imprint of the cross, "the conformity of the cross"[6] and the "cruciform" life of God,[7] in which Christ's suffering and death creates the possibility of ever new and ever lasting life for every person. This is the hope in which I live; the hope that my life joined with others might be lived for others and might participate in giving life to all through Christ's own love.

6. Moltmann, *Experiences of God*, 72.
7. Moltmann, *Trinity and the Kingdom*, 121.

5

Somewhere between Zion and Bryce
(The Livingness of God)

SUMMER ROAD TRIPS ARE by nature an adventure. The road ahead beckons us into the unknown, introducing us to a future that lies around each new bend, sometimes it delighting us and sometimes putting us to the test. My fourteen-year-old son and I learned this as we joined another father and son on a seven-day road trip to Utah exploring the canyons of Zion and Bryce National Parks.

Our sons were classmates at school and over the school year our families had become close. While we were comfortable sharing family time together, the prospect of traveling with one another stirred a bit of apprehension in all of us. Consciously for the fathers and perhaps subconsciously for the sons, we knew that finding a way to work through normal agitation and disagreements would not be easy. As fathers we anticipated that conflicts would occur that would either draw the four of us together or push us apart. We also recognized that the manner in which we worked through these struggles would greatly affect each teen's ability to forge closer and more mature relationships. With great hope that our bond as fathers and sons might be deepened, we set out on the road together.

In retrospect I should not have been surprised when three days into the trip, a late-night scuffle broke out between the boys. That day the four of us had completed two of Zion Canyon's most strenuous hikes. In the morning we followed a trail several thousand feet up to explore the beauty of Hidden Canyon. In the afternoon we ventured into what is called the Narrows, trekking through a canyon so narrow at its base that at times we found ourselves hiking in the river itself to find a passageway through. By the time we finished, we were exhausted.

Weary yet amazed at all we had experienced, we reminisced about our day's adventure over dinner and afterwards all I could think about was elevating my feet and getting some rest. Not more than ten minutes later a loud knock on the door and shouting in the hallway announced that a conflict had erupted. One look at our son's faces and we knew just how serious it had become. After several minutes of angry accusations, the argument dissolved into a steely silence that persisted overnight.

At breakfast the boys' facial expressions and body language matched their glum one-word responses. By the time we began the two-and-a-half-hour drive to Bryce, lines had been clearly drawn. As dads of young teens it felt like watching a contest to see who could remain silent and look the most miserable the longest. Their obstinacy pervaded the car. Half an hour into the morning's drive, the other father unexpectedly pulled over and announced that we all needed to get some fresh air. He suggested that we all take a short hike.

Predictably each son headed in different directions, walking at such a fast pace that it sent us fathers scurrying to catch up. As I walked behind my son I took the time to pray. The longer I prayed the more I realized that I needed prayer just as much as my son. I had gotten quite frustrated and impulsively wanted to intervene, to put an end to this mess, but I knew I was in no mindset to effectively do so. As we walked, the path narrowed and we began following a circular ridge of sandstone that was leading us ahead. Making our way around this massive rock enclosure, we could see it leading to an overlook of the whole landscape below. Just as we stepped onto the overlook, our travel companions stepped in from the other side. Without warning the two boys came face to face. Surprised by this unexpected meeting and clearly not ready to talk with one another, each boy turned around without saying a word and walked in the opposite direction. Disappointed at the squandered opportunity which destiny had so wonderfully provided, we followed our sons back to the car to continue our journey through the arid beauty of southern Utah in silence.

It was painful to be in the presence of such conflict. I was frustrated that my fellow chaperone was holding me accountable not to step in. Uncomfortable with my own powerlessness I became so restless that my caffeine addiction flared up. All I could think about was a cup of coffee. I gruffly looked at the map to see how far it was to the next gas station and when we finally (finally!) arrived I leapt out of the car, handed my son a ten-dollar bill, and uncharacteristically said to him, "Get anything you want."

I made a beeline for the coffee dispenser and waited impatiently behind a rather short stocky woman who was between me and my caffeine relief. Without looking at me she said in a fairly loud voice, "This is the third thermos that is empty, I guess we are out of coffee." Attempting to control my own impatience, I responded, "Right when I really need a cup." Turning around as if she had expected someone else to be standing behind her, she took a good look at me while I took a good look at her, and we smiled, amused over our shared need and disappointment. The possibility of a yet-to-be-identified connection beckoned me, and I looked more deeply into the person standing before me. In that brief moment I saw the kind face of an Asian American woman some years past middle age, out in the middle of Utah on vacation. I sensed she was trying to share a little bit of wonder with those around her while her spirit was still open to what comes next. Unexpectedly, I recognized in this stranger so different from me the very longing I had in me but to this point was unable to share with my own traveling companions.

Now I don't usually strike up conversations with people I don't know, especially when I am agitated like that, but something about this woman elicited a question. "Are you coming from Zion and going to Bryce, or are you coming from Bryce and going to Zion?" Without the coffee we had come for, we found ourselves in a fifteen-minute exchange where she told me about Bryce and I told her about Zion. She then went to get her sister and her sister's friend asking me to tell them about our adventures in hiking the Narrows. The conversation absorbed our attention as it meandered to include vignettes from vacations long ago. Following some time of listening to one another and laughing together, the coffee man finally arrived with a thermos full of fresh-brewed coffee.

Back to our original mission, we filled our coffee cups, took a few sips together and then like relatives we took time to individually shake each other's hand, bowing just a bit and wishing each other well on our respective journeys. As I began to walk away I glanced up and caught the eye of the woman who I first encountered. As we passed she softly said to me, "God bless you." Like a brief thundershower of rain falling unexpectedly on a bone-dry desert, I felt myself refreshed and awakened to a deeper connection that the two of us had been sharing all along. As I responded, "And God bless you," it was confirmed in me that my deepest longing was not for coffee but for sharing, sharing the goodness of life as God created it to be. What I was truly craving was fellowship, and God's gracious willingness to restore fellowship with and among us.

As we drove away and I continued sipping my coffee, I pondered the refreshing nature of our interaction. Drawn to the women's vivacious spirits, I found myself in a very different place. Suddenly I felt fortunate to be out on the road with our sons, driving from Zion to Bryce, even if they were locked down in a standoff and silence still filled the air. For me the silence was different now. It was no longer empty but now was filled with the memory of the woman's smile and a love springing forth from God, which she had shared with me. The vitality of God's presence within this woman's spirit was passed along and the joy of sharing a childlike anticipation of what lies ahead remained as a gift within me.

As we drove toward Bryce and they drove toward Zion, I wondered if she remembered my smile and if she too had experienced something life-giving in our interaction as we waited for coffee. The more I reflected upon what had taken place, the more I felt my anxiety, my agitation and even my sense of impatience being contained by something beyond me. Instead of being locked out and at odds with myself and with the life I wanted to live, I found myself drawn in, caringly embraced by a power that made me joyful to be alive. I don't know if my conversation partner sensed herself being encompassed by God's life-full presence as I did, but I do know our unexpected encounter continues as an example to me of the new life God desires to share with us. Certainly the One who came and got my attention that day did not bring coffee, but a vitality of life that took hold of us and shared with us its goodness.

Jürgen Moltmann identifies this life-giving power as "the creative livingness of God"[1] through which the Holy Spirit raised Jesus from the dead into God's eternal life. What distinguishes Moltmann's understanding of the life-giving power of the Spirit is that this power is the life of God. The Holy Spirit is the well spring of God's life, distinctively acting in conjunction with the Father and the Son as the source of life on earth and in every person. This was the source of the shared life that came alive in my coffee companion's interaction with me. It awakened me to the living fellowship that "the life force of the Spirit" seeks to share.[2]

As the vitality of God's life in the Spirit touches those divided by conflict, diminished by injustice, incapacitated by violence or threatened by death, "the life force of the Spirit" creates opportunities for people to be set free to experience the love of God's own fellowship. It is this love that engenders hope,

---

1. Moltmann, *Trinity and the Kingdom*, 123.
2. Moltmann, *Spirit of Life*, 89.

breaks down walls that divide, and facilitates the sharing of life that is reflective of the triune God's life of love. The Trinitarian life is lived in, with, and for the other. Out on the road, as our relationships were suffering the degradation of conflict and its accompanying ill will, the livingness of God was at work to create a different narrative for our summer journey together.

Moltmann's own experience as a German soldier and prisoner of war exemplifies the power of the livingness of God. While in a World War II prison camp, Moltmann encountered victims of Nazi aggression, aggression of which he had been a part. Though he was burdened by the shame of sharing in the disgrace of the Holocaust and full of despair, he and other German soldiers were visited by a group of Dutch Christians, and he remembers, "I was frightened at the prospect of meeting them, because after all, I had been at the front in Holland, during the fighting for the bridge in Arnheim. The Dutch students told us that Christ was the bridge on which they were coming to meet us and that without Christ they would not have been able to speak a word to us. They told us about the Gestapo terror in their country, about the killing of their Jewish friends and about the destruction of their homes. But we, too, could step on this bridge which Christ had built from them to us, even if only hesitantly at first, we could confess the guilt of our people and ask for reconciliation. At the end we all embraced. For me it was an hour of liberation. I could breathe freely again."[3]

The power of God's livingness creates opportunities for new life for those entrapped by personal conflict, oppressed by injustice, overcome by violence, or victimized by the atrocities of war. Embraced by the Spirit, encompassed and indwelt by the life of the crucified and risen Son "new energies for living awaken in us" a new spirit of community in which they are held together by the Spirit's life and love.[4] The opportunity to receive this living fellowship is ever new, continuously providing a foretaste of the new creation to those drawn together.

3. Moltmann, *Broad Place*, 34.
4. Moltmann, *Source of Life*, 24.

Somewhere between Zion and Bryce, I unexpectedly experienced myself being released from the power that had so effectively divided our two sons, paralyzed the two fathers and diminished our relationships. While the division we experienced was not rooted in physical harm, its power had exceeded our abilities to cast it off. But a taste of connection and the newness of life shared with the three Zion-bound travelers awakened the life of God in me and opened me again to the hopeful and shared life which God has begun to create anew in the world.

Indeed while the boys remained in a lockdown, entrapped by the finality of needing to be right, their story was not the only story being told. While they measured themselves against each other and in the eyes of their fathers, all of us—including the women I met—were being measured against the suffering love of God in Christ. Fearing condemnation the boys had committed themselves to defending their honor to the end, as if domination or defeat were the only possibilities available to them. Yet in the midst of the conflict a new destiny emerged. Once I was released from my own fear that the entire road trip would be ruined by conflict, I was given confidence that the future held new opportunities for all of us. Having tasted life-giving connection with three strangers, I was confident that a new bond not of our own making would be made available to us.

Released of my sense of hopelessness and confident about the future, I "traveled lighter." Spiritually free I conversed in the front seat as if we weren't locked in misery and dueling in silence. I remember my friend looking at me as if to note that something had changed and then immediately responded in kind. We talked as friends for the next hour or two. When we arrived at our cabin, just over the ridge from Bryce Canyon, we joked and worked together. We spoke with each other and to each boy with a love that we had longed to express to each other when the road trip began.

That afternoon, I invited one boy at a time to go fishing in the stream that meandered through a meadow near our cabin. Each caught a small fish and after reeling it in, hurried back to the cabin to proudly present it to the other father and son. It didn't matter that the fish were less than 8 inches long; the livingness of God was spreading. When both boys later asked me if I would take them out fishing again, I looked first at one and then the other and said with a smile, "Why don't you go out there together?" They paused. One nodded, and then the other, and soon with fishing poles in hand they headed back out to the meadow friends once again. In that moment, we experienced the life of the Spirit making us a part of the living fellowship of God.

6

Saint Elizabeth's New Community
(Out of Nothing—Creation)

WITH TWO PREVIOUS CONVICTIONS and a nine-month rehabilitation program at the state's expense, Elizabeth knew she needed just the right arguments to convince the judge not to sentence her to the recommended maximum twenty-four months in prison. She sat alone on the floor of her jail cell rehearsing the words she planned to speak before the judge. Elizabeth worked to refine the arguments that had previously convinced even the most seasoned judges that this well-educated, forty-three-year-old white business woman, wife, and mother was the exception to the rule. Her well-structured litany of excuses echoed off the walls as she stared aimlessly into the darkness of the drain just a few feet in front of her. Day after day, hour after hour the sound of her own voice was her only companion.

Experience taught her to emphasize the fact that her son needed her. She would make the point that now, during his early adolescence, it was important for a mother to be home, important to be able to pick her son up after school so that he didn't get involved with the wrong crowd. Of course she would not mention that she herself was the wrong crowd, and that for the past eight years as her drug use accelerated into deep addiction, her husband Chris had been doing most, if not all, of the parenting. With twenty-nine years as a cameraman for a major television network, Chris had earned the right to work regular hours and arranged his life so that he could take their son to school every morning and pick him up afterwards, a task his mother couldn't manage.

Over time Elizabeth had lost all credibility with those closest to her. Her deceitful action had taken a toll on her relationships. But in front of the judge she knew how important it was to spin a web of lies into a single thread of clearly expressed testimony. She recognized that the outcome she was working to achieve rested on her attention to detail. How she held herself in the courtroom, the way she articulated her words, the eye contact she made all were important in convincing the judge that she had command of her inner self, and after all she had been through, she had turned herself around. Rather than attempt real change, she practiced exchanging the truth for a lie. Over and over again she rehearsed every word, every gesture to insure that her masterful charade could continue. It was, however, in the midst of one of Elizabeth's well-chosen, confidently spoken, impeccably articulated sentences that a voice appeared out of the jail cell drain and declared, "Elizabeth, stop! Stop wasting your life!" Midsentence her words came to a sudden halt. Nothing visible changed yet seemingly out of the dark void of the drain came a voice that quieted her words and quelled the constant flow of her obsessive thinking.

As the voice seized her attention, Elizabeth felt beckoned both by the power of the dark void in front of her and by the words she had heard. The empty darkness frightened her while the voice stirred in her a longing she had abandoned many years before, a longing to be known and drawn close. Startled by the clarity of the voice, her momentary pause was unexpectedly filled with memories. The voice reminded her of the protection she had received long ago in the darkness, when as a five-year-old girl God had chased away the nighttime ghouls and goblins from underneath her bed. Though the stakes were much higher now, Elizabeth's choice was made. She would fix her attention on the voice that spoke her name and revealed the truth about her life. Later she testified, "In those moments I was given hope and I knew that my life was heading in a whole new direction."

When hope rises out of the hopelessness of our own lives, its presence witnesses to a source of assistance that knows our weakness and points us to a power greater than ourselves. Elizabeth clearly associated this hope with God's authority over wrongdoing and his willingness to bring renewal into her life. Moltmann reminds us that Christ's resurrection from the dead overcomes the finality of death, making possible the regeneration of life and life after death for all who will receive it. Just as the natural world was created "ex nihilo," out of nothing, so Moltmann maintains that the new future, created out of the cooperative work of all three persons of the Trinity is also created "out of nothing."[1] Out of the emptiness, the nothingness of Elizabeth's jail cell drain, the voice spoke with such command that it convinced Elizabeth that her opportunity for new life sprang out of a power that was operative in the midst of the darkness. Mysteriously, she was convinced that this power was able to create what Elizabeth trusted would become thoroughly new. In the weeks and months that followed, Elizabeth began to taste the Trinitarian triumph of God's suffering love creating first hope, then freedom from the past, and finally energy for a new future.

Moltmann recognizes that the resolve that prompted God to create the world out of nothing is the same resolve that prompted God to send the Son into the world to liberate it from sin and death, inaugurating the new creation through the outpouring of the Holy Spirit. Stated simply, God's essence of love and his unconditional affirmation of life form the resolve to create all things anew.[2] Moltmann often reminds his reader of two fundamental truths about God: Because God is

1. Moltmann, *God in Creation*, 91.
2. Moltmann, *Source of Life*, 88.

love, God refuses to let die those he created; and God loves life and thus seeks to regenerate it by sharing his own eternal life with those he created. Through acts of self-sacrifice, all three persons of God resolve to set people free and to create room for them within their Trinitarian fellowship. As believers are drawn into the fellowship of God by the appearance of hope and love out of nothing, they taste what Moltmann describes as the three persons of God existing "with one another, for one another and in one another."[3] They witness that there is "space for a full unfolding"[4] of the distinctive abilities of all three persons of God. Similarly they discovered that there is room in this fellowship for the "unfolding" of the new creation within and among them as they experience the mutuality of care, which the three persons of God provide. Such care is transformative, for it is the exchange of the life-giving love of God, the love that creates out of nothing.

While Moltmann describes the work of the new creation as a cooperative work of all three of the persons of God, the Son is identified as the one in whom the new creation takes place. The Son, "the image of the invisible God and the firstborn of all creation (Col 1:15)," emptied himself of power by coming into the world in human flesh. He suffered "the God forsakenness of sin and death"[5] and died "an eternal death"[6] for all. As the Son suffered and died he gathered up the nothingness of death, the destructiveness of injustice, the alienation of every person from God, and the sorrow, pain, and the isolation of those lost. In his death, the annihilating power of death was broken. Out of love for every person, the Spirit raised the Son out of death as "the first born from the dead" (Col 1:18) so that through the supremacy of his new power he might become "the living space of believers and their space in the new creation."[7] Together the

---

3. Moltmann, *Coming of God*, 298.

4. Ibid.

5. Moltmann, *God of Creation*, 91.

6. Moltmann, *Trinity and the Kingdom*, 80.

7. Moltmann, *Sun of Righteousness, Arise!*, 166.

Son and the Spirit beckon every person and draw the willing simultaneously into the nothingness of the Son's death and into the newness of his resurrected life.

As the Son makes room in himself for the sinful and the Spirit draws them into this new living space, the new creation dawns. Held within the Son, the Holy Spirit breathes new life into sinful people, instilling hope that leads ahead. Out of nothing and from nothing, those held within the Son begin to be made new. Remarkably the new in them resembles nothing of the old. In Moltmann's words, the new "is unique and eternal and never returns again" for it looks ahead to the beginning of a complete new life.[8]

Out of the void of her jail cell drain God's presence welled up in the darkness as a new space in which Elizabeth could dwell and a new place in which her old way of life could be made new. Drug addicted, defiant, and unrepentant, Elizabeth was given a living space into which she could grow and in time be transformed by the care of God's life-giving love. This love stirred hope within her that she might have a new beginning with her family and that she might make amends to those she had wronged. Elizabeth's efforts to begin the process of reestablishing her relationships led her to reach out to a whole series of new people. I was among those who were brought into Elizabeth's life.

Elizabeth sought me out as a pastor to help her face the truth about herself. For Elizabeth the truth included the unrepentant arrogance that had allowed her to construct a life built on lies, deceit, and betrayal. In reading Paul's first letter to the Corinthians, Elizabeth identified herself not with the outcast or the lowly but with "the things that are not" (1 Cor 1:28) that God chose to create anew. In the wisdom of the cross Elizabeth's sinfulness became her pathway into Christ's death and resurrection and thus the means by which she was included in the new creation of all things. Elizabeth found hope in the non-existent, the things yet to be. At first she was not able to explain why—in

8. Moltmann, *Source of Life*, 28.

her shame—she felt so much joy and why this difficult time in her life was so full of expectation. As the weeks and months passed, she realized that through the very deficits of her own character, she had access to a newness of life that sprang out of the nothingness of Christ's death. For Elizabeth, out of "the things that are not" Christ was bringing "the things yet to be." Out of Christ's death sprang a new sense of self for Elizabeth and a new and everlasting relationship with God.

Elizabeth's experience is mirrored in Moltmann's own experience. Yet more aptly "the things that are not" in Moltmann's wartime experience involved the loss of life and the finality of death. For Moltmann the dawn of a new day sprang out of the darkness of death, turning "humiliation into new hope."[9] As a World War II Prisoner of War facing his own complicity in the Nazi atrocities Moltmann discovered himself companioned by the Christ who himself suffered condemnation and death. He writes, "I felt growing within me the conviction: this is someone who understands you completely, who is with you in your cry to God and has felt the same forsakenness you are living in now."[10] As One who was present with him, the crucified and risen Christ was dwelling in his despair and invisibly taking action on his behalf. He writes, "I began to understand the assailed, forsaken Christ because I knew that he understood me. The divine brother in need [is] the companion on the way, who goes with you through this 'valley of the shadow of death,' the fellow-sufferer who carries you with your suffering."[11] This divine brother is the forsaken Christ who has been raised from the dead, bearing in himself "a living space" created out of the nothingness of death to carry in himself the lowly, despised, despairing, and hopeless into a new set of possibilities.

As the crucified and risen Christ inwardly companioned Moltmann, the transcendent nature of his experience testified that Christ was at work creating a new way forward out of what

9. Ibid., 4.

10. Moltmann, *Broad Place*, 30.

11. Ibid.

is not. Moltmann testifies that set free from the disgrace he carried, he experienced himself carried forward into a truly new space, which held for him a truly new surprise. He writes, "But that made it possible for us to live with the guilt of our own people, the catastrophes we had brought about, and the long shadows of Auschwitz, without repressing them and without becoming callous . . . I discovered that in every end a new beginning lies hidden."[12] This was for Moltmann the hope of the new creation of all things springing up in him out of nothing. This insight undergirds Moltmann's understanding of hope and his unwavering faith in the future. The one who has overcome death patiently waits to whisper hope into the finality of life in this world. By a power of life rising within and around us we are drawn forward in a new mutuality of life, which we share with God and each other.

None of us expect that out of emptiness, out of the end of our capacities the triune God would share hope and an ever-expanding experience of new life. What is astonishing is that this new beginning cannot be grasped. It cannot be taken hold of or acquired. In fact we don't experience it. It experiences us and then we receive it as a gift in our emptiness, in the end of what we do.

Moltmann's experience as a POW confirms this. He was unable to access the experience of being comforted by God through his own capacities. Moltmann writes, "But whenever in my despair I wanted to lay firm hold on this experience it eluded me again, and there I was with empty hands once more. All that was left was an inward drive, a longing which provided the impetus to hope."[13] Moltmann points to our experience of the new creation springing up out of death, out of things that are not, out of our incapacity to make ourselves new. Into empty hands, hearts, and lives the triumph of God's suffering love brings first hope, then new life in Christ, and then the initiation of the new creation of all things.

12. Moltmann, *In the End—the Beginning*, 35.
13. Moltmann, *Experiences of God*, 8.

Moltmann grounds his understanding of creation out of nothing in "the open Trinity." Out of the generosity of God's openness springs ever new and everlasting life. By throwing open the life of the Trinity to every person and community[14] the fullness of God's creative powers is released through the distinctive work of each of the three persons of God and the cooperative nature of their unity. Moltmann recognizes that the uniqueness of this Trinitarian work broadens the scope and deepens the reach of God's creativity. He recognizes that as people are held in the living space of Christ in the fellowship of the Holy Spirit, a profound transformation is begun both within them and in their connection with God and with others. God's way of living for others (the way of sacrificial love) and in others (the way of mutuality, of sharing oneself with others), begins to come alive in them.[15] What is begun is indeed a wondrous way of being both in God and with one another.

Elizabeth's experience of this new connection with God and others awakened in her a new "social space" in which she soon discovered there was room for her husband, her son, other suffering people, and eventually a new church family. From the first moment she was addressed by God in her jail cell, Elizabeth's focus was on the future that God would provide. As Paul proclaims in Romans 5:5, the hope that God placed in her did not disappoint.

In fact four nuns visited her jail cell the very day that the voice rose up out of nothing. Their support led her to an AA group whose members encouraged her to continue to yield herself to the care of the "Higher Power." Three weeks later, covered by prayer, the judge heard Elizabeth's confession and rejected the maximum sentencing recommendation. Within a month Elizabeth was living at home with her husband, Chris, and their son. God continued to provide resources to fill the empty spaces. Two weeks later Chris brought home an invitation to a Bring-a-Friend Sunday at a coworker's church, the

14. Moltmann, *God in Creation*, 242.
15. Moltmann, *Coming of God*, 301.

church where I was serving. The invitation lay on the kitchen countertop for a couple weeks until at Elizabeth's initiation, the couple attended worship. Several of us at church recall this family's first Sunday. Their eyes bore witness to their sorrow, but their faces were alive with anticipation. They came empty handed, longing to be filled. Thanks be to God, that Sunday and every Sunday morning they left worship walking ahead into the open space of the new creation which was dawning in and around them.

A New Contagion

(The Force Field of Love)

VIOLENCE IS AN EPIDEMIC in the community surrounding our church. It is a contagious disease. Like a virus, it reproduces, setting off a cascade of violent acts. The news of the shooting death of another high school student in our area sent fear rippling through our multiethnic community. This particular gang-related shooting occurred less than a mile from our church. Families in our congregation knew the victim and while we were well aware of the danger that teenage boys face in our neighborhood, we were shocked that this particular young man had been targeted. He wasn't involved in a gang and to make matters worse, the murder was clouded by the fact that the victim was a twin. Questions of mistaken identity deepened the heartache and complicated the grieving.

As pastor, I felt that the tragic nature of this shooting must be brought to the attention of our congregation. It was a stark reminder of the entanglement of human sin and the work of evil in our community. I included it in my Sunday sermon and asked the congregation to ponder how our church might respond. In the next several days, gang retaliation began as expected, and fear began to paralyze our community. The victim's family discovered that not one church large enough to host the expected funeral crowd was willing to open their doors. In addition to being overwhelmed by grief, the family members found themselves burdened by a sense of shame that they could not find a church to come around them in their time of need. When the family inquired about the possibility of our church hosting the funeral, we met with them and brought the request before our leadership.

The leaders of our church were in the midst of a yearlong exploration of the reconciling power of the Lord's Supper. Increasingly they were becoming aware that the power that drew them into fellowship with God and with each other was also drawing them into fellowship with our neighbors. While processing the ethical implications surrounding communion, our leaders weighed the request to host the funeral. After security concerns were addressed, the elders unanimously gave their approval, knowing that their decision would test the congregation's capacity to practice fellowship, hospitality, and reconciliation in a whole new way.

Tensions were high the morning of the funeral. Outside the sanctuary a SWAT team of well-armed police was hiding just out of sight. Inside, down the center aisle, an open casket rested in plain view. Large groups of students filled the back of the sanctuary while small groups of students bustled back and forth, some to glimpse, others to touch the young man's body who—just days before—had been full of life. As the sanctuary filled to overflowing, so did the emotions of the students. Sobs and wails could be heard throughout the sanctuary and those expressing sorrow were deeply disoriented by the loss. Unprepared for the finality of death, students who went forward to view the body returned to their friends overwhelmed with grief and disturbed by injustice. As the din of student voices rose, an occasional shriek of panic could be heard, followed by a sudden outbreak of commotion as individual students rushed to flee the sanctuary. Fear, anger, and sorrow permeated the space where we had gathered. What had entered the sanctuary was not only the bullet-ridden dead body of a young man but the pervading power of death to snuff out hope in our community.

As a seventeen-year-old in World War II, Moltmann also lived through the cessation of hope in his own community. As conscripts in the German air force auxiliary, he and many others endured night after night of bombings in their hometowns. They watched civilians die and lost many of their own. They were forced to climb over charred bodies to put out fires, witnessing the devastation of whole neighborhoods. One particular day, while standing next to his dear friend Gerhard Schopper on the platform of their anti-aircraft battery, Moltmann was knocked down by the explosive force of a bomb. Rising to his feet he looked for Gerhard only to find his friend's body; Gerhard's head was torn off and missing. Later while serving as a German infantryman, one of Moltmann's companions was mortally wounded and died in his arms. As if more grief could be added, six months after becoming a prisoner of war, he and his fellow German prisoners saw photographs of the Belsen and Buchenwald concentration camps and were confronted with the role they had played in perpetrating Hitler's reign of death. Moltmann writes, "Slowly and inexorably the truth seeped into our consciousness, and we saw ourselves through the eyes of the Nazi victims."[1] "Left alone in that place of death," Moltmann began to ask the question he has asked throughout his life, "Why am I still alive?"[2] His despairing question was not unlike those that were haunting the mourners at our church that morning.

When it was time to open the service, I extended the comfort and love of the risen Lord Jesus Christ to all who were gathered. I spoke about the faithfulness of the Lord to attend to every sorrow and to share new life with all who will receive it. As the service proceeded, hymns were sung, prayers were said, and remembrance after remembrance was shared, but it seemed that nothing could penetrate the darkness that filled the

1. Moltmann, *Broad Place*, 29.
2. Ibid., 17.

sanctuary. Every word that was spoken seemed to bounce off a wall of despair.

All throughout the service the victim's twin brother sat emotionless in the front row. Rarely did he open his eyes, as he remained unresponsive to the remembrances that were shared. Neither friends nor coaches who took time to greet him before and during the service were able to rouse much of a response. At first his posture seemed defiant, but as I studied him I began to wonder what effect the trauma of his brother's death was having on him.

Looking through the eyes of others has been Moltmann's lifelong mission, whether they are the eyes of Holocaust victims, the German civilians who died in eastern Hamburg or of his dear friend Gerhard. As a twin brother myself, I could not help but look through the eyes of this teenager and see the emotions that were running through him; the rage he felt, the bottomless sorrow he faced, the intolerable emptiness that surrounded him. To this point in the funeral, my focus had been on leading the service, but as I watched him, a sense of empathy shifted my focus. Viewing him through the eyes of a grieving twin brother, I recognized that he was still in shock and to a large extent was unaware of all that was taking place around him.

When I stood up to deliver my planned eulogy, my mind was not on the remarks I had prepared. After delivering the opening paragraph, I looked at him and could not continue speaking. I felt drawn specifically to address this twin brother's pain. In silence I put aside my eulogy. Looking out at the largely African American crowd, I said, "I bet you are wondering what I am doing here, and why I am officiating at this service." Pausing again to gather my thoughts I said, "As I speak I sense that I have been called to lead today because I myself am a twin and I am to extend, one twin to another, whatever companionship I can." As soon as the words left my mouth, the eyes of the living brother sprang wide open. As our eyes met, the dividing walls of age and race had already crumbled and I felt a deep connection to this twin brother who I was just beginning to know.

I spoke spontaneously about the bond that twins share and the profound comfort twins have in each other's presence. I shared about the indomitable love and trust that twins share with each other and how, in the teenage years, life without your brother is simply unimaginable. I then reiterated what many others shared about his brother's faith and said, "I know that at this very moment your brother is filled with hope that you will now walk the same path he walked, and that God will lead you ahead." As I spoke out of a place of deep empathy, the power of God's hope seemed to narrate its story within him. His eyes came alive and as they reflected new life, God's empathetic love that began between two twins began to spread like a contagion to all who were gathered.

As those present witnessed the birth of such an unlikely connection, a new sense of life and love circled the room. As I experienced it, I recognized that I too had been drawn into the hopelessness of death and made a part of the trauma of the twin brother's despairing heart. Yet as I began to connect with his pain, the Spirit of the living Christ made himself known as the hope of new life, first in me and then the despairing twin. As this change in energy circled round the sanctuary, an audible sound accompanied it. People stirred in their seats and teenage voices could be heard breaking the silence. Sensing a new spirit, I concluded the eulogy by assuring those gathered that Christ's resurrection provides life stronger than death, and urged them "to step out of the darkness and into the light." I invited each one to receive as a blessing, "the love and life of God in them." After I sat down, my colleague gave a call to faith to step out of the darkness that had taken a precious life and into the light that promised restoration. Over half of those in attendance stood up in response. Many students provided their contact information that day, and in the days that followed over fifty of these students began a new relationship with our church.

God's force field of love was experienced as a multisensory power that came upon those gathered like a wave of vitality. The power that first awakened an empathetic connection between two strangers quickly embraced the sanctuary with love and strengthened those present to bravely walk ahead. In just a few moments, many were released from despair and filled with God's own hopeful life. A foreboding evil was replaced by the Spirit, exchanging anxiety, fear, and despair with empathy, connection, and hope. The empathetic love of God drew together all who were present and provided us a glimpse of a new future. New relationships were born, and a new ministry formed with area churches to support those who experienced the unexpected spread of God's hope and love at the very center of despair.

What we witnessed that day was a release of the unconquerable love of God. Moltmann identifies this "vitalizing field of force" as "the pull of [the Son's] self-giving love,"[3] which sets people free from the finality of death. Moltmann recognizes that the Son's surrender into death is so powerful that it draws all those who are willing "through death" and into the new life the Holy Spirit provides. Therefore Moltmann rightly concludes that nothing can separate us from the love of God, which is in Christ Jesus.[4] What we experienced flowing in and around us was what Moltmann identifies as the triune God's "heartwarming stream of love" coming upon us as a "gale of wind which seizes hold" of our future and begins to enact it in the present moment.[5] Some consciously, others subconsciously, experienced the love of the Father, Son, and Holy Spirit as empathetic life springing out of death.

Moltmann recognizes that all three persons of the Trinity participate in triumphing over the powers of evil and death. Stated simply, he explains that God's investment of himself in the life of the world is a Trinitarian venture of love. As an act of love, God resolved to overcome the powers of death and to create the world anew, transforming the perishable into the imperishable and the fleeting into the eternal kingdom of God. This love forms a "vitalizing" force field, which both draws and indwells

---

3. Moltmann, *In the End—the Beginning*, 69.
4. Ibid.
5. Moltmann, *Sun of Righteousness, Arise!*, 167.

people in the present with glimpses, tastes, and traces of God's own "livingness." Set free from the spirit of annihilation, many mourners who gathered at the funeral were emboldened by a new energy within them to join with others in extending the love of Christ to every member of our community.

The theological connection between the love inherent in God's self-sacrifice and its life-giving effect is indeed complex, yet the lived experience is not. When my eyes first connected with the twin's eyes, love abounded. We did not ask for such a love and we certainly did not produce it. As the bereaved brother's pain momentarily became a shared sorrow, what burst forth was compassion and affection. It was a gift that God gave us, and we tasted it together. As we experienced it, so did many others in the sanctuary. It is Moltmann's conviction that only through love are people set free from the destructive power of death, for love is a participation in the life of God. Moltmann writes, "In the field of force of God's love, earthly created, human life becomes eternal life, which participates in the living God."[6] First as empathy, then as freedom, and finally as community, the triune God's love begins a metamorphosis from despair to hope, enabling God to dwell in this world and this world to dwell in God.

The hopelessness of Moltmann's war experiences witness to the same force field of God's love in the midst of horrific suffering and death. His personal discovery of Christ's solidarity with him when he felt most forsaken grounds his hopefulness and empathy for all the suffering and forsaken in the world. As a POW, Moltmann experienced himself "held up from afar" and his broken-heartedness unexpectedly healed.[7] Decades later he acknowledged, "We received what we had not deserved, and lived from a spiritual abundance we had not expected."[8] It led him not only to the cross of the Son, but also to the Spirit's vitalizing wellspring of life and to the self-sacrificing Father's care. Together these three draw both victims and perpetrators

6. Moltmann, *Experiences in Theology*, 147.

7. Moltmann, *Experiences of God*, 8.

8. Moltmann, *Broad Place*, 33.

forward into God's own future fulfillment. Through what he terms "Trinitarian Thinking" Moltmann identifies the shared work of the Trinity to be the source of the new creation, which includes victims and perpetrators, oppressed and oppressors, the dead and the living.[9]

Paul's promise that "the one who began a good work among you will bring it to completion in the day of Jesus Christ" (Phil 1:6) is what gives Moltmann confidence that everyone will receive the opportunity to be remade and recreated in the image of God. He writes, "If God is God, even violent death cannot prevent him from doing so. So I believe that God's history with our lives will continue after our deaths, until the completion is reached in which a soul will find its wrongs redressed."[10] Embraced by a force field of love that extends beyond death, Moltmann's thinking becomes inclusive. He writes, "I am thinking about the lives of those who were unable to live and were not permitted to live: the beloved child who died at birth, the little boy run over when he was four, the 16-year-old friend torn to pieces at your side by the bomb that left you unscathed—and the countless people raped, murdered or 'liquidated' . . . [Those who] die a premature, violent and by no means affirmed death, like the millions of young people in my generation who died in the Second World War."[11] In the new creation, which is the fulfillment of the force field of God's love, all will be given the opportunity for new life in the community of God.

As a part of that same community, those in the sanctuary that day who grieved the senseless loss of a young man's life were set free from the paralyzing grip of violence, despair, and death. Freed by the force field of God's empathetic love, those present retain within them the seeds of imperishability and hope. Through the in-reach of God's empathy, these seeds are planted into every person's experience and grow, like a new contagion, into opportunities for new and everlasting life.

9. Ibid., 288.
10. Moltmann, *In the End—the Beginning*, 117.
11. Ibid., 116.

8

The River Walker

(The Way of Jesus Christ)

LIKE PILGRIMS RETURNING TO Zion, we fathers and sons returned to Zion National Park, which had amazed us the year before. We went as the psalmist has proclaimed, to "walk about Zion, go around her, count her towers, consider well her ramparts" (Ps 48:12). As we set out, we were unaware that just around a bend, not in the road but in the river, we would walk in the light of God's presence. This year we ambitiously set our sights on hiking "The Narrows," a sixteen-mile stretch of the Virgin River Canyon whose red sandstone walls tower above the winding river.

So much had changed in a year. Both boys, now fifteen years of age, were taller than their fathers and surprisingly, could not stop talking to one another. They had forged a friendship that allowed us to relax in each other's company. As we looked ahead, none of us realized just how rewarding our time in Zion would be. I felt like the psalmist who declared, "Blessed are those whose strength is in you, who have set their hearts on pilgrimage. As they pass through the Valley . . . they go from strength to strength, till each appears before God in Zion" (Ps 84:5–7).

The truth is that even before we began the trek through the Narrows, we had a lot to learn. Fortunately for us the learning began the night before at the Wagon Wheel Restaurant just outside the park. As it turned out, our waiter was an experienced hiker and each time he returned to our table he told us more about hiking the Narrows. He said, "No one makes it down the river without the proper river boots and walking stick." He then told us that our walking sticks—two-and-a-half-inch thick shoulder-height poles—were our friends and that with their help we would be able to traverse the most swiftly flowing sections of the river. He then assured us, "There is a technique that you learn as you hike the river. There is a whole cadre of experienced hikers who see themselves as expert 'River Walkers.' If you see one of them you will know it." Overwhelmed with a little too much information, we smiled and paid the bill.

Out on the river the next morning, things became clearer. When the water rose above our knees and the currents became strong enough to whisk us downstream, our poles functioned much like a third leg. Just like our waiter had said, each of us discovered a river walking technique through trial and error. Soon all four of us agreed that the best technique for traversing the swiftly flowing sections of the river was to face into the current, firmly plant our pole up stream and then put a good portion of our weight on it. While it seemed odd to face our bodies away from the direction we were traveling, breaking all forward momentum, we did so out of fear of being overcome by the rushing river. Each of us found it to be a necessary sacrifice so that we might use our strength to find stability before risking a step across the forceful currents. The tripod of our two feet and the pole created the stability we needed to push off and venture another step. Mile after mile we found our way down the canyon, all the while heavily depending on our poles to secure our footing. We found this technique to be quite tiring and slow. We safely made it across the river, but we didn't make much progress down river toward our destination. After a full day of hiking, we finally reached the halfway point of our trek and made camp for the night.

That evening while discussing the important role that our poles had played in helping find our way down the river, my pastor's mind recognized a metaphor for "walking by faith" in the correlation between hikers putting weight down on poles and believers resting lives on the promises of Scripture. In both cases, finding our way across dangerous currents depends upon our ability to rest the weight of the future on the support of an outside source of stability. Certainly those new to the journey of faith—as well as to river walking—need this support to help them stay upright while attuning themselves to the new terrain.

As I lay in my sleeping bag that night, I considered the limited strength and endurance we each had. I asked myself if our technique was the most efficient way of traversing the currents. Were we expending too much energy by continuously facing into the current and then striding laterally? Was there a way to safely move with the current as it tumbled toward our destination? As the night wore on, exhaustion won out and I went to sleep under the stars hoping for a new way to walk.

The next morning the canyon put us to the test. For the first four or five miles the riverbed was filled with large boulders, some as large as houses. They forced the river to abruptly turn, and when it did, it deepened and rushed with greater force. Within the first hour of walking we found ourselves hiking through cold, waist-deep water. The chill of the night air lasted well into the morning and sunlight would not reach the canyon floor until almost noon. While we laughed when it happened, all four of us walking along in single file encountered the same deep hole in the riverbed and momentarily disappeared from sight, submerged in the water. At the time we shook it off and pretended that being soaked from head to toe could not keep us from reaching our destination, yet we were well aware that we had to continue hiking just to keep our body temperatures up. Concerned about the boys I noticed that their faces had begun to lose color and their bodies got the shakes every time we stopped for a snack. No matter what we did we could not get warm. Trudging along at an increasingly slower pace, our eyes were focused down the canyon where in the distance the sunlight appeared to reach the canyon floor.

After almost three hours of hiking, we came to the longed-for bend in the river around which we finally stepped into sunlight. Overjoyed I threw off my pack, fell to my knees, and lay on the ground soaking in the warmth of the sun. After double-checking to see that all four of us had made it into the sunlight, I let go of the responsibility of guiding our party down that portion of the river and my mind drifted off into a bit of a stupor. Haphazardly I gazed upstream just in time to see a swiftly moving figure emerge from behind the canyon wall. I lifted my head to get a better look and striding before us was a tall shirtless young man with long sinewy arms and big broad legs, high stepping his way down the river. As he passed effort-lessly, I knew this was what our waiter had told us several nights before. This was a Master River Walker.

As I watched, I witnessed an entirely new way of trekking down the river. Only occasionally did he use his pole to steady himself. He was so confident that his gaze fell out ahead of him. Like a kayaker reading the river, he determined the angles of his descent by using the river's power to his advantage rather than fighting against it. Never did he face into the current to plant his pole up stream, rather he employed his pole to set his direction and occasionally to steady his steps. From that moment on, my memory of him gave me a vision of how I was to walk without fear as I traversed even the strongest currents and the deepest water. Just that brief glimpse of him made me a better walker for it taught me a way of finding solid ground when at first all my feet could find were slippery rocks. While I couldn't see him for long before he disappeared around a bend of the river, a vi-sion of his movement remained with me and gave me hope for finding a new way of walking.

Like many young people in the church, I was taught to "walk by faith" and to "lean on the promises" of Scripture like the walking sticks we held in our hands. We were taught that if we properly employed those promises they would help us advance in the kingdom of God. While in principal I was taught to trust in God, I lived as if everything depended on my timing and strength to make it across the rushing currents of sin and death. As time passed and I struggled to maintain the Christian walk, I began to doubt that I had been taught the best technique. Leaning on the promises of God with my own strength and depending on my own timing wasn't working. Too often something went wrong on the journey, and I ended up abandoning "the crossing" in the midst of the swiftly flowing waters. But as I came to know the Son in connection with the Spirit and the Father, I learned to travel across the dangerous currents trusting his life to well up within me, come around me, and draw me ahead into his way of walking. In this wondrous new way of being in Christ, the responsibility and power for reaching the destination remained with him. As I released my grip of control, the power of Christ's love and life pulled me forward.

I have discovered that in walking this way, the power that surrounds and dwells in Christ resists the strength of the currents that are coming against me. I am not asked to resist such powerful forces, but to allow myself to be beckoned and drawn by the power of the Spirit which surrounds and dwells in Christ. The Spirit's power draws me into Christ as he crosses through the dangerous currents of sin and death that remain in the world. As I have been drawn into Christ, I have discovered the power of Christ's own life and love welling up in me strengthening me not to resist the currents but to remain in Him. In his life and love I experience him as a wounded companion, sympathetic to my fear and empathetic toward every person's suffering. As the Spirit beckons me to walk encompassed in Christ, and Christ's life and love well up within me, I experience the gathering of all things in the fellowship of God—Father, Son, and Holy Spirit. Suddenly the deliverance of God works in conjunction with the dangerous currents as the Master River Walker strides through them. Encapsulated and indwelt in the purposes of God in Christ's death and resurrection, I am drawn together with the whole kingdom of God not toward the end of life but to its everlasting fulfillment. In and with the Master River Walker I walk with others downstream, headed not across the river but toward the final destination of the union of all things in the life of God.

Jesus Christ is the one who has been sent into the world by the Father and raised by the power of Spirit "with healing in his wings" to walk against every current of temptation, every form of sin, every bastion of injustice, every onslaught of evil, even the onslaught of death itself. Overcoming all that works to destroy life, he is every river walker's deliverance for he walks not only with us and around us, but he walks within us and us in him. Through the living hope he places in us, we are to bravely walk ahead. As the prophet Isaiah declares on behalf of God,

> Do not fear, for I have redeemed you;
> I have called you by name, you are mine.
> When you pass through the waters, I will be with you;
> And through the rivers, they shall not overwhelm you . . .
> For I am the Lord your God. (Isa 43:1–2)

The risen Christ traverses troubled waters and shares his power, his suffering love, and his indestructible life with all those who will receive it.

Moltmann identifies the crucified and risen Christ as one who "is already on the way to redeem the world and to establish his rule."[1] Entering the finite world entrapped by the power of death, the crucified and risen Christ is accompanied by a "lifefull space" into which he will gather those willing to travel with him. In glimpsing Christ through prayer, people of hope are drawn into this life-filled space and begin to learn how to walk anew with the risen Christ. Moltmann explains, "The way of Christ comes into being under the feet of the person who walks it. To tread the way of Christ means believing in him. Believing

---

1. Moltmann, *Way of Jesus Christ*, 32.

in him means going with him along the part of the road he is taking at the present moment."[2]

Walking in the way of Jesus Christ thus means participating with Christ as he fulfills his messianic mission first to the poor, the oppressed, the neglected, the sick, the suffering, and to sinners. It means attending to the magnetism of the living presence of Christ welling up in those seeking to walk by faith. For Moltmann this is much more than just applying "a theory about Christ" or putting ones weight down upon a scriptural promise in order to exert one's own effort to live out Jesus' mission. For Moltmann it is following the way of life of Jesus Christ "in which people learn who Jesus is, learn it with all their senses, acting and suffering, in work and prayer."[3]

The way of Jesus Christ is always with us and he beckons us to walk with him into the future. We do not conjure up his way of walking, nor introduce it to ourselves. Moltmann teaches that Christ's "intensive life"[4] comes around and in us at every new moment. The intensity of his life lived for others is known in his suffering. He suffers our sinfulness, our pain, and our own suffering with and for others. He suffers the sinfulness of those around us and their pain and their suffering with and for others. Through his suffering the powers of sin and death are broken and Christ shares that victory with everyone who will receive it. This allows those willing to walk by faith to dwell in other's suffering through empathy and prayer and to begin to share in the victory Christ has won. Moltmann recognizes that those walking in the way of Jesus Christ participate in God's "mutual indwelling" of believers,[5] and as a form of prayer, participate in Christ's suffering for others. As we are held in Christ and Christ in us, believers participate in the "gathering together

---

2. Ibid., 33–34.

3. Ibid., 43.

4. Moltmann, *Coming of God*, 291.

5. Ibid., 307.

of all things," and in carrying them forward into a time when "all things will be redeemed."[6]

For Moltmann the life of contemplative prayer is experienced not apart from the world but with it and in it. As believers "linger" in Christ's presence they are lingering in his "livingness."[7] It is in this lingering that the eternal life-fullness of Christ bears the fruit of new life in believer's attitudes and actions. Not through the exercise of their own power but through the grace of being beckoned and opened to the wondrous presence of Christ in this world, believers taste the full-filled life and then bear witness to it in their actions. As the Apostle Paul has written, receiving the free gift of grace makes believers "instruments of righteousness" in this world (Rom 6:12–14).

It is thanks to Moltmann's encouragement that I have made contemplative prayer an integral part of my personal and professional life. As the father of young adults, I struggle to love and honor the independent men my sons are becoming while also remaining a source of trustworthy guidance. Our son recently made a decision that disturbed me and because it impacted our family life, I felt compelled to oppose it. As I reasoned about it with my wife, who felt I was taking too harsh of an approach, I was moved to participate in indwelling prayer for him. In prayer I entered into Christ's deep love for our son and became aware of Christ's suffering love for him. As I abided there, I could not help but desire to suffer for and with my son, even given the reality of our disagreement. If Christ was willing to suffer for him, my deepest desire was to do the same. As I discerned in my son's heart the profound love of God in Christ, I was moved to allow this same profound love into my approach to myself, my son, and to all I encounter. As I participated in Christ's indwelling presence, I changed and my actions changed.

Through contemplative, indwelling prayer we can be drawn into Christ's deep empathy for the hurting, the outcast,

6. Moltmann, *Way of Jesus Christ*, 284.

7. Moltmann, *Coming of God*, 291.

and the sinful. This form of prayer also draws us into the liberation Christ has won through his suffering for all of us. While it may be difficult and painful to live with decisions made by those we love, what I was surprised to learn was that the experience of indwelling prayer demonstrated to me the depth of Christ's love for me, my son, and all people. It was out of this depth of love that I found strength to love our maturing son with compassion.

Moltmann's own life bears the fruit of "lingering" in "the presence of eternity" not for weeks or months or even years but for decades. Beginning in the later half of his sixth decade and extending now into his eighth decade, Christ's new life in him has surprised him. He has become "young and lively again."[8] He writes, "Whether we are young in years or are growing older, we are always standing on the threshold of our possibilities. Sometimes it takes a little longer to become young and to seize the possibilities with delight and love."[9] As the life of Christ indwelt him and he indwelt Christ through lingering prayer, Moltmann experienced a reversal in the aging process. He compares himself to an age-old tree, gnarled, all but dead, which blossoms and puts forth unexpected fruit. Personally and theologically Moltmann's life bore and continues to bear new fruit over the last three decades. Fresh insights and a love of the future led to the writing of volume after volume after volume. Feeling young and lively, the pace of this prolific theologian quickened.

As we lay exhausted on the shores of the river that day in Zion, drenched from having sunk so deeply into the crevasses of the river bed, we realized we had unnecessarily born the burden of river walking under our own power and wisdom. Fearful we might not make it and suffering the early stages of hypothermia, we were ready to open ourselves to the Master River Walker's wondrous way of walking.

As I open myself to the Master's way of walking I realize that my own knowledge and trust in the Word can lead me no

8. Moltmann, *Broad Place*, 334.

9. Ibid., 285.

further. Only a new way of walking, modeled by Jesus Christ will lead me ahead and join me with those being saved in Zion. The Apostle Paul assures us in Romans 11:26–27, "Out of Zion will come the Deliverer; he will banish ungodliness from Jacob." "And this is my covenant with them, when I take away their sin." In the warmth of the Son's radiance, my inner being was cleansed, my sins were washed away, and I was prepared for the new life of the Master River Walker dawning over all the earth.

9

A Wondrous Way of Being
(A Shared Sociality)

FROM THE FIRST TIME I met Edith, I knew. I knew that the Lord Jesus was alive in her and that the kingdom of God was flowing through her. The energy of God's love had so penetrated her that all she encountered experienced God's goodness streaming through her. I met Edith at the door of our church following a Christmas Eve service. With "Joy to the World" still playing, she emerged with twinkling eyes and a radiant face declaring with authority, "Pastor Mark, I give God praise and thanks for the birth of our Savior, born this night a baby, Emmanuel, 'God with us!'" Without pause, she stepped forward, shed the authoritative mantle of her words and gave me a big hug.

As a white pastor serving a largely black congregation for nearly ten years, I had learned to adapt my ministry to the cultural norms of our faith community. I had learned to expect warm greetings from African American parishioners and more importantly, to recognize the authority of those whose ministry rose out of the anointing of the Holy Spirit. I had learned how to test out that authority and then to follow its leadership. Even on that first night I could sense God's power drawing me to

Edith, setting me at ease and dispelling the distrust that so often divides those of differing cultures. As we shared the joy of God's incarnation, I trusted that the bond we shared was a reflection of the hopeful dynamics of the coming kingdom. While on Christmas Eve we carried different cultural histories and knew different sides of the dividing wall of racism, the hope of Emmanuel's future was drawing us together.

For the next seven years Edith and her husband, Tim, graced our church with their ministry. Much could be said about the ease with which Edith did ministry, but what set her apart was the way she prayed. When Edith prayed, I felt the prayers of the saints gathering around her and at times praying through her. In the resonance of her voice the cries of her ancestor's suffering could be heard. In the conviction of her spirit she carried forward the unbroken struggle against racial injustice. There was a joyful godliness about Edith and every time she prayed, whether it was for the needs of an individual or against the most intractable forms of discrimination, she prayed with hope. Edith's prayers were founded on the conviction that in Jesus Christ, God has the last word and that last word is "life everlasting."

For Edith, prayer covered everything. Every misstep, every hurtful wrong, every destructive act, personal tragedy, or social atrocity was drawn into the hope of God's coming kingdom in prayer. Praying for the impossible was what Edith believed God was calling every Christian to do. In fact, when Edith really "got to prayin'" her deepest sorrows yielded the highest praise for they revealed the power of God's undying love. According to Edith, prayerfully standing on God's promises opened the faith community to God's healing touch in the world. Opportunities for singing and praying with Tim and Edith were like feasting at the banquet table of the King, tasting a piece of the perfection that is yet to be.

Unfortunately, both Tim and Edith's health began to decline simultaneously. It seemed unfair that only a few weeks after Tim suffered a debilitating stroke, Edith suffered a stroke as well. While Tim was still hospitalized, Edith was able to remain at home and when I heard the news of Edith's stroke I immediately called and arranged a visit. As soon as I stepped through the door I noticed that Edith was struggling to walk and was using a cane. Closer observation revealed that there was a significant amount of paralysis on the left side of her face and in her left arm and leg. Very, very slowly we found our way into the living room. While Edith spoke slowly and with a slight slur, she was excited to tell me about a prayer time she had the day before.

An acquaintance, a Central American woman, had stopped by unannounced the previous day and asked if she could pray with Edith. Apparently while they were praying, a "visitor" as Edith explained it, entered and remained in the room. At one point "the visitor" began walking around the two women, and it was at this time that Edith sensed "a healing come upon her." As I listened intently, I sensed that the blessing of the experience was still unfolding so I invited Edith to pray. Moving my chair closer to hers, I took Edith's left hand in my right hand and knelt down on one knee in front of her.

I began by thanking God for the healing that he was bringing in Jesus Christ. After I prayed, Edith prayed. While she was praying I noticed that the longer she prayed the clearer she spoke. Wondering how this could be I opened my eyes. As I did her voice fell silent, her eyelids fluttered, her furrowed brow quivered and then all at once her face relaxed as if God's peace had fallen upon her. Humbled to be in the presence of the Lord, I closed my eyes and waited to see what was coming next. What came was a touch of glory that bore witness to the unity of God's presence, and I was included in it—Edith, the Holy Spirit, the Son, the Father and me. I knew I was to be still and to allow the presence to pass through. As it did, I sensed that a restorative power was on the move. Grateful to be included I knelt on both of my knees in front of Edith while still holding her hand and silently giving God thanks. When I finished praying we lingered in silence with our heads bowed.

To my surprise the silence was broken by a sudden outburst of laughter. When I looked up, Edith's head was tilted back and she was boisterously laughing right out loud. She was laughing like she was outdoors sitting in the shade at a family picnic on a hot summer's day. Initially I was perplexed as to what had caused such an abrupt change in Edith's disposition and what could possibly have taken place that caused Edith to laugh so loudly. Fearing she was not laughing with me but at me, I felt myself recoil. Before I could respond, Edith lifted my right hand up in her left hand, and exclaimed, "Who would have ever thought that a white man would be kneeling in front of me, praying for my healing?"

Not knowing for sure whether Edith had just declared a victory for God's reconciling powers or whether she simply was expressing her amazement that the man who had journeyed with her into the throne room of God was white, I remained silent. Yet a holy presence within me drew my attention to how high above our heads Edith had raised our hands. Amazed by how high they had been raised, I sensed God was not allowing me to focus on my defensive feelings nor Edith to dwell on the ethnicity of the man whose hand she still grasped. Rather we were to focus on all that God had done. Sensing this, Edith and I fell back into prayer. Each of us thanked God for his healing touch and praised him for the blessing of having been given the other as a companion for such an intimate experience of his fullness. Still grasping hands, I sensed no tension between us, only gratitude. Yet when I released Edith's hands and I looked directly at her, a sense of discomfort rose up in me revealing how embarrassed I was at having focused on our racial and cultural differences. I thought we trusted one another, yet what had just taken place exposed a residue of racial tension and a mistrust that could not be overlooked. It made me wonder what this was all about.

Was I suddenly dealing with fears and suspicions I thought I had released long ago? Were long-buried wounds, vestiges of resentment and fear, arrogance and prejudice rising up in and around us as our "round-trip prayer flight" landed back into the everyday world? I was sad to think that an active resistance to the deep inner connection that the Spirit had given us might reside in me and threaten all that God had done within us. In prayer we were partners, co-travelers drawn into the healing presence of God. But outside of prayer, fears seemed to have surfaced and I wondered if I had momentarily fallen into the historical social fabric of the larger community where racial stereotypes and injustice still divide. What we did know was that the healing love of God had been poured out upon us. I also recognized that to fully integrate our doubt and fear with our gratitude and love, something more needed to be faced.

In the days that followed I reflected upon my own experience and in doing so acknowledged the unexpected difficulty I had encountered. My unexpected discomfort became a stark reminder of the "unmistakable dissimilarity" of our lives to the fully reconciled life of God.[1] After standing in the light of God's regenerative presence with Edith, I recognized that nothing about our relationship could cast aside God's healing love. Not even my unwillingness to be free from the past had prevented God from drawing me into a new unity with him and Edith. As I pondered the fact that God was and will be with us and in us, I concluded that God was giving me a new opportunity to be healed.

Moltmann teaches that "the open Trinity" overflows with life-giving love and continuously shares with believers the "reciprocal indwelling" of the life of the three persons of God. Just as each person of the Trinity reciprocally dwells in and shares life with the other two, so the three persons of God beckon and draw believers into their "open, inviting and integrating unity."[2] This unity provides believers a wondrous new way of being together in which no one suffers alone and new life is an opportunity afforded to everyone. This unity also enables

1. Moltmann, *God in Creation*, 61.
2. Moltmann, *Sun of Righteousness, Arise!*, 156.

believers to share with each other the same life and love they receive from the three persons of God.

This sharing creates a new kind of life, which is both distinctively individual and communal. Moltmann insightfully understands this new kind of life to be an experience of sociality and "the network of social relationships in which life comes into being, blossoms and becomes fruitful with others."[3] In this new kind of life, individuals retain their individual identity and consciousness while sharing consciousness with other believers and with the whole faith community. Indwelt by God's empathy and love, believers not only feel what another person feels, but begin to co-experience another's life as their own. It is a wondrous way of being embraced by the life and love of the triune God.

Moltmann describes the sociality of the believing community's consciousness as an ability to move outside our selves and be wholly present with and for the other. "The Trinitarian concept of community envisages *diversity in unity* from the very outset . . . for differentiation is one of the essential elements in community."[4] For Moltmann the distinctiveness of every individual is to be recognized as a part of the community's strength, not just for what the individual adds to the community but also for what the community does in and with the individual's weaknesses. Held in the "diversity in unity" of the Trinity, the individual's weaknesses become the diversity, the otherness that God makes room for and commits to overcome.[5] Moltmann understands this living space within the Trinity to be a "social space of reciprocal self-development," a space in which the sinful are remade, transformed, and "develop" into a reflection of God's way of living for others.[6]

The Apostle Paul describes this holding of other's weaknesses "carrying in the body the death of Jesus, so that the life

3. Moltmann, *Spirit of Life*, 219.
4. Ibid., 221.
5. Ibid., 219.
6. Moltmann, *Coming of God*, 301.

of Jesus may also be made visible in our bodies" (2 Cor 4:10). As the believing community carries our weaknesses and we participate with the community in carrying other's weaknesses, we are in the present moment, participating in the future transformation of one another as we share God's ability to indwell one another. Through prayer we can dwell in and with others and participate in their liberation, healing, and transformation. Indwelling prayer is the wondrous new way of being together in and with the triune God. Through this indwelling prayer no one in the believing community suffers alone and every member participates in the development that becomes a part of the new creation of all things.

This was the blessing that Edith and I shared in prayer. From the very first day I met her to the day I was drawn into her healing, Edith allowed me to taste the mutuality of her life with the triune God. Initially she shared with me the dignity of being a child of God, rescued from the degradation of racial injustice and filled with a generosity of spirit toward all who seek God. After her stroke, she shared with me the exhilaration of being physically released from paralysis and the well-being that naturally follows. After her healing we shared with one another the new space that God provided, which could hold our discomfort in sharing the intimate moments of healing with a person of a different race and culture. In this new space, the disconnection of historical and present-day racism could be reconciled and unity could be made familiar as a part of our new life in and with the triune God.

In looking back at our experience I recognized that as Edith grasped and raised our hands, black and white together, they were raised above our heads not just as sign of physical healing but a sign of the healing of the wounds of racial prejudice and injustice as well. What I experienced provided me "traces" of the fulfilled life to come.[7] God had gone before us and as I glimpsed his unity, provided room for my doubts and fears, my residual prejudices, and my complicity with in-

7. Moltmann, *God in Creation*, 135.

justice. Stated simply, there was and is room for sinfulness in the healing intervention of God.[8]

Through the sacrifices of the Father, the Son and the Holy Spirit, what still divided Edith and me was being integrated into the life of God.[9] What disconnected us from God and each other became a part of the shared hope that, in the fellowship of God, we might be fully liberated and redeemed. What rose within me was the hope that all God has eternally accomplished could be fulfilled in our relationship. In Moltmann's words, trusting means "seeing the world in the advance radiance of God's future and living life here as a foretaste of God's fullness."[10]

The encouragement of seeing our lives in the advance radiance of God's future provides the believing community the vision it needs to remain hopeful. Such hope enables the believing community to trust that the traces of the new creation it experiences in physical and social healing are indeed foretastes of the power of God's self-sacrificing love, which will one day overcome all that divides this world. The effects of hope create a bridge on which every person can cross the gap between our imperfect practice of faith and the perfect promises of faith, between our weaknesses and the "strength through weakness" on which God has established the future. It is a bridge on which the suffering, the despairing, and the dying can walk. The power to walk is not their own, but is God's power hidden in the hope that at the end of ourselves, a new beginning is already present.[11] On the bridge people have the opportunity to discover their hope becoming "a living hope," filled with God's "livingness," which makes everything new. This hope refashions relationships, overturns injustice, reconciles enemies, and swallows up death. Moltmann assures us that as this begins to happen "we don't just experience life's natural energies; we also

---

8. Moltmann, *Coming of God*, 28.

9. Moltmann, *Trinity and the Kingdom*, 83.

10. Moltmann, *Sun of Righteousness, Arise!*, 184.

11. Moltmann, *Coming of God*, 234.

already experience 'the powers of the age to come' (Heb 6:5)."[12] As these powers are deployed, hope that encouraged, beckoned, and drew people into God's embrace now bursts forth with the resolve to call into being things that are not. They create a wondrous new way of living in which every person can participate in the new creation of all things.

The embrace of God's hope encompasses all of earthly life like a cocoon. This embrace encompasses all that is yet to become what it was created to be. It embraces the combination of fleeting aspirations, failed efforts, separation from God, separation from one another, disintegration of life, and death itself. This combination is truly dark, disordered, and messy, yet as the triune God indwells this miry bog of death, hope pervades every aspect of life in this world. What emerges from the indwelling of God is more than just a new set of choices, or the gift of transformation and eternal life for a few. What emerges is the possibility of living hope for all.

What emerges from this cocoon is true metamorphic change, new possibilities for every person and for all of creation. Embraced in time by the hope of God's life-giving love, every person's story becomes a hope-full story waiting to be fully told. No one's life is excluded. New possibilities emerge in the physical, the spiritual and the social life of every person. Life has become hopeful, for what has emerged is not essentially spiritual, heavenly, individual, or private. The metamorphosis of the Christian life is communal, reciprocal, public, and radically new.[13] What emerges is reflective of the fellowship of the Triune God's future, which is a shared celebration of God's life in human flesh, and human life in God.

What has emerged from the embrace of hope has, is and will come to all of us. Let it come. Let it indwell, unite, change, and give us life with and in the triune God. There is little to do until it is done to us. We do not change ourselves. We release ourselves. We do not exert ourselves or fashion ourselves. We

---

12. Moltmann, *Sun of Righteousness, Arise!*, 77.

13. Moltmann, *Trinity and the Kingdom*, 123.

submit ourselves to be united with God, to be open as God is open and then to become a part of the new creation of all things. Receive the embrace of hope and wondrously it will become a living hope that joins us together with the future of the triune God. Be embraced.

——— 10 ———

Flying Round Trips
(The Movement of Mutuality)

WHEN HOPE LETS US glimpse the future in Christ, it can be like flying round trip to a new destination without having to leave home at all. For those traveling by air, two different places, two sets of people, two entirely different contexts are experienced in the very same day. Air travelers enter an airport in one reality, time zone, and community and "magically" exit airport doors in an entirely new location, a new time zone, an altogether new reality. Similarly, those traveling by hope experience two "places" and two "time zones," seemingly traveling between the temporal and eternal, a round-trip journey without even leaving the ground.

As my mom's health declined over a period of eight months, I took several round-trip journeys to Colorado to be with her. It had been my mom's decision to be transferred from a hospital to a hospice toward the end of those eight months, and it was her desire to share her final journey with my three siblings and me. While I don't think any one of us were prepared to intimately share what we were so reluctant to face, Mom would have it no other way. It didn't take long to realize that when we stepped into the hospice facility we were taking a step out of our world and mysteriously into another where the human journey through death was fully accepted.

After Mom's first night in the hospice, my brother and sister volunteered to take the first shift of accompanying Mom on her new journey. Little did they know as they greeted her that she had already completed her first round-trip flight. As they stepped into her room they both sensed that she had been waiting to tell them something important and after quickly greeting them, Mom got right to business. With her eyes mostly closed, she said, "I don't want to go ahead with this, they are . . ." She stopped and then began again, "I don't want to go ahead with this, they are . . . they are . . . they are . . ."

My siblings naturally thought she was referring to the nurses, doctors or the hospice facility as a whole. But after a time of futile guessing, Mom finally added, "They don't speak English there and they are trying to keep me from speaking."

Not clear about what she might mean or how to respond, my sister simply replied, "Mom we will look into that for you. Brian is a lawyer and he is good at these kinds of things and he will look into it."

They were onto something. Mom replied in kind, "Now Brian, make sure you look into the fine print."

Keeping in step with Amelie's approach, Brian responded, "I definitely will, Mom, but it might take some time."

Later that morning when I arrived at the hospice, Brian informed me about the earlier conversation. Together he and I entered Mom's room, but even before I could sit down she picked it right back up again. Without opening her eyes, she asked, "Well, did I do the right thing?"

Assuming that she was asking about her decision to come to hospice, I assured her, "Yes, I think you did."

"Well, have you heard from my lawyer?"

Noticing a change in the tone of my mother's voice I grew concerned. Sensing her apprehension about the future I sat down and boldly responded, "No, I haven't but I did hear that it might take some time."

As I was worrying to myself, she adamantly objected, "Well, they don't speak English there and I don't want to go!" This response made me anxious. As her son I naturally wanted my mother to feel at peace, and the resistance I sensed made me afraid that I would have to convince her to stay in hospice care or that we would need to figure out where to go next. Fortunately something clicked in me and my pastoral-self realized that I didn't yet know the depth of Mom's resistance. Familiar with these sorts of conversations at the end of life, I knew my job centered on listening for the feelings behind the words. Adopting my mother's storyline I replied, "Mom, I don't really expect them to speak English up there."

"Well, I don't want to go there if they don't speak English."

Taking note of mother's second stubborn refusal, I found myself battling my own feelings of empathy and sorrow. Yet my desire to respond to her fear drew out of me my next response. Seeking help, I released myself into God's companionship and trusted that my words would help broaden her perspective and beckon her toward hope. Not completely sure of what I was about to say, I heard myself confidently proclaim, "Mom, they don't speak English there, they speak from the heart; it is from their hearts that they communicate."

She paused and considered this, "But it is so different there."

"I know it is different. It is different there, because it will change you."

"But I don't want to change."

This time without thinking words flew out of my mouth from a wisdom much beyond me. "But it will change you because it is *so good*. It will change you *for* the good. Yes, it is different up there. *Because* it is so good, it will change you."

While that response slowed her down for a moment, it didn't prevent her from issuing yet another objection. "But I want to be an American there and speak English."

"Mom you can't be an American there, you've got to be the Lord's." As the words came off my lips I sensed that I was giving my mom over to a future I was not going to share. Sensing my own loss I was overcome with grief and unable to speak. Brian who was still standing behind me with his head and hands raised up in prayer spoke for me, "*God's . . . she can be God's.*"

"Yes, Mom, you can be God's." There was a brief moment of silence and then I asked, "Do you want to be God's, Mom?"

When an answer was not immediately forthcoming, neither Brian nor I filled in the empty space but patiently waited for Mom to think it through. When she answered her voice was full and clear. She stated simply, "Yes."

Attentive to our mother, my brother and I watched as the resistance seemed to fall away, and fear was replaced by peace. In that moment I recognized in her a contentment that so many times before had witnessed to God's presence and to her joy in the beauty of life in this world. Now it seemed to be leading her ahead. As her sons, my brother and I were no doubt saddened to lose our mother's spirited presence, yet to our surprise we were rejoicing in the journey she had already begun to take. Staying present with her as she hovered between two realities, we sensed that we were being beckoned by hope to "travel" beyond the here and now. What drew us ahead was an energy that began to fill the room. As it did, I rose to my feet as I felt the presence of God. Captivated by joy, my brother and I were drawn into silent prayers of thanksgiving. Our rejoicing however was short-lived, for our silence was broken by yet another of mother's objections. She was still troubled by the place she had traveled the night before.

"But they write and speak so very fast up there. I can't write that fast!"

Again with words that seemed to be given to me I responded, "Like lightening. From the heart you can write and speak like lightning."

"I don't have to speak Arabic do I?"

"No, Mom you don't have to speak Arabic, in fact you can think in English and speak from your heart. You have been very good at doing that for a long time now." Pausing briefly I added, "You'll be alright."

And then taking a deep breath she said, "Well . . . alright."

With those words of acceptance, it felt as if the ceiling of the room opened and the weight and power of God came down upon us. Overwhelmed by God's presence, both Brian and I fell onto our knees next to our mother's bed. Time seemed to slow down, and for a brief moment, we hardly knew where we were.

Admittedly, experiencing life in this world "as at once" life in the age to come is paradoxical.[1] Moltmann explains this paradox as the mutual indwelling of shared love where, "in love God throws himself open to become the dwelling space of those he has created, and those he has created take God in themselves."[2] I believe this is what took place in my mother's hospice room that day. The hope of God's love beckoned the three of us by the Spirit into Christ's resurrected life. Together we experienced what Moltmann describes "as at once mortal *and* immortal," "transient *and* intransient" and "temporal *and* eternal."[3] The three of us took part in what was and what will be. As we did we sensed that the hope we experienced had the power to draw us from one reality to the other and back again. The power of the resurrection was not restricted to life beyond this world but also resided in the very present hope that allowed us to taste the fulfillment that only unity with God could bring. Into this fulfillment and into God's care we released our mother, rejoicing in the future that we had glimpsed.

Looking back, I can't help but recall how gentle and yet powerful God's presence had been. While we couldn't have known this at the time, we were witnessing the full embrace of God in human flesh drawing her in, preparing her for the descent into death and journey into new life. Overwhelmed by the implications of saying goodbye to Mom, we were speechless. With tears of gratitude flowing down our faces we recognized

1. Moltmann, *Coming of God*, 71.
2. Moltmann, *Sun of Righteousness, Arise!*, 95.
3. Moltmann, *Coming of God*, 71.

that God was reshaping Mom physically, emotionally, and mentally. We had been privileged to help prepare her for the transition from the perishable to the imperishable, from the fleeting to the eternal. The experience of journeying with her in the power of hope convinced us that the finality of death is no barrier to God's work of regeneration. It persuaded us that the power of God's new creation was at work in Mom. It was then and is today close at hand for my brother and me.

Jesus made it clear that the union he experienced with the Father is the same hope-filled intimacy that the believing community can experience when surrendering to God and one another in love. Jesus prayed for us, "As you, Father, are in me and I am in you, may they also be in us . . . Father, I desire that those also whom you have given me, *may be with me where I am, to see my glory*, which you have given me because you loved me before the foundation of the world" (John 17:21–24). Flying round trip is the commitment to surrender in hope to the crucified and risen Christ, to see his glory and then become a reflection of that glory back to the world.

Moltmann's description of mutuality beautifully describes how my Mom, brother, and I had unexpectedly "traveled round trip" that day. We experienced the mutuality of the love of the Trinity, which was palpable in Mom's hospice room. While our conversation had been disjointed at times, it had great significance for it helped unite Mom with a new community; Moltmann calls it "the community of Christ."[4] What a privilege it was to love and be of service to Mom in this way. No greater honor could be given to us than to be chosen to beckon our own mother into the kingdom of God and for us to experience the eternal life of God residing in her.

The experience she shared with us was of the eternal life of God, yet she was holding to her temporal identity, fearing the changes to come. As God's love led us to help her work through her fear, there was no division between our physical lives and God's eternal life. God's indwelling love embraced

4. Ibid., 231.

us all. Even Mom's ailing physical body and her resistance to a new union did not prevent God from sharing the movement of divine mutuality with us. For Moltmann transformation is not only a spiritual transaction. It takes place through the mutual indwelling of God in the lives of his people. The eternal God is to become our dwelling place and our earthly lives his eternal place of dwelling. Moltmann writes, "We shall not be redeemed *from* the earth . . . we shall be redeemed with it. We shall not be redeemed *from* the body. We shall be made eternally alive with the body."[5] The understanding that we are in God and God in us shapes Moltmann's personal encounters with suffering as well as his journey of faith. It is much of what forms his love for God.

What a gift it is that Jürgen Moltmann has shared his private practice of the two great commandments of Jesus. He was moved to do so after reading Augustine's Confessions in which Augustine answers the question, "But what do I love when I love you?" Moltmann's response reveals his journey of opening himself up to the mutuality of God's indwelling love.

> When I love God I love the beauty of bodies, the rhythm of movements, the shining of eyes, the embraces, the feelings, the scents, the sounds of all this protean creation. When I love you, my God, I want to embrace it all, for I love you with all my senses in the creations of your love. In all the things that encounter me, you are waiting for me.
>
> For a long time I looked for you within myself and crept into the shell of my soul, shielding myself with an armor of inapproachability. But you were outside—outside myself—and enticed me out of the narrowness of my heart into the broad place of love for life. So I came out of myself and found my soul in my senses, and my own self in others.
>
> The experiences of God deepen the experiences of life. It does not reduce them. For it awakens the unconditional Yes to life. The more I love God, the more gladly I

5. Moltmann, *Source of Life*, 74.

exist. The more immediately and wholly I exist, the more I sense the living God, the inexhaustible source of life and eternal livingness.[6]

Just as Moltmann describes it, my mother, my brother, and I discovered God waiting for us as we faced the finality of death. By choosing to share the intimate details of her descent into death with her children, Mom was cooperating with God who waits to whisper the hope of eternal life into our stories. What we glimpsed was Mom bringing her vulnerable thoughts and experience before the community of God in her children,[7] and we experienced the redesign of human life in the image of the Trinity. In the image of the shared life of the Trinity there is no place for the autonomy of one over another, no room for personal agendas, no room for the pride of nationalism. Mom's pleas to hold onto her identity as an American and to speak English in the new community were vestiges of her old way of life. By God's grace, Mom's willingness, and our gentle nudges of love, the bonds that tied her to her old way of life began to fall away, and a new way of being was instilled in her.

"Flying round trip" is an extraordinary experience, but one that is open to all who live in the hope of the resurrection. In this hope God remains present with the suffering and he is present to free and draw them into the joy of sharing life with him and others. As we witnessed Mom opening herself to the embrace of God's love, we too experienced the joy of such an exchange for ourselves. What we witnessed firsthand was the power of God's surrendering love that beckoned Mom to surrender herself into death that indeed she "might be raised to the newness of life."

As the community of faith travels in the Spirit, believers are given the Spirit's power to reflect Christ's love for others in their actions and to live as signposts of the deliverance from violence and injustice in this world. What we witnessed that day in Denver was deeply personal to our family, but the mutual

6. Moltmann, *Source of Life*, 88.

7. Moltmann, *Kingdom of God*, 119; Moltmann, *God in Creation*, 92–93.

indwelling does not stop there! As the community of faith experiences God's love individually and together, we are then called to reenter life in this world prepared to stand with the forsaken and in solidarity with those suffering from injustice. In bearing the image of Christ's love for "the other," the returning community recognizes there are no solo flights. All who travel do so together; changed by the mutuality they share with the triune God. Flying round trip with the community of faith is done with an ever-widening diversity of people, all brought together by the loving embrace of the triune God. Moltmann reminds us, "The enjoyment of God is not reserved for the solitary soul. Those who rejoice in God will also rejoice together. They perceive each other in God and recognize each other as members of the all-embracing divine community of all things."[8]

After the intensity of the experience seemed to pass, I said, "Mom, my heart is so tired now, I need to stop and rest, and you can rest too."

"Yes, you rest, and I'll rest."

After a moment or two Brian said, "God is good and he is trustworthy to lead you ahead."

I repeated his words with a slightly different emphasis on the verbs. "God *is* good. He *will* lead you ahead."

And then from a very content place within her our mother said, "Alright now . . . Bye."

She waved her fingers to us and we said, "Bye bye, Mom."

"Bye bye, boys."

"Bye bye, Mom."

With that she fell into a deep sleep. As my twin and I left her room, we reentered life as we had known it. While we walked into a new journey of grieving our mom's absence, we walked with assurance that she was on a one-way journey toward a hope-filled destiny prepared for her in Jesus Christ. Thanks be to God, one day we'll go too.

8. Moltmann, *Sun of Righteousness, Arise!*, 185.

$$-11-$$

An Impending Peace
(Many Stories, One Destiny)

WHAT DREW THEM WAS basketball played on summer nights under the lights of a neighborhood church parking lot. At first they just seemed to put up with the "Great Promise of Scripture" that the twenty-one-year-old program director / referee shared while they cooled down with a cup of ice water and a snack. But increasingly the teenagers responded to what they heard, sharing fragments of their own stories. Summer basketball grew into a year-round youth group when nine of the teenage boys, both Hispanic and African American, kept showing up. The older boys shared more and more of their own stories during discussion time, revealing challenges they faced. When news broke that one boy's parents were divorcing, the other boys compassionately came around him. They asked if one of the young adult leaders and I could meet privately with him. We did and our bond as a group deepened. The sharing soon revealed that the majority of the boys had experienced some form of displacement in their lives.

As relationships with the boys grew, the leaders were moved to share their own stories. Veronica, a twenty-two-year-old Japanese American woman, revealed her frustration at being unable to fully engage the central commitment of her life, promoting peace within the community in which she grew up. Veronica's own great grandparents came from Hiroshima, and as a Japanese American she recognized that she survived the American bombing that killed so many of her distant relatives. She described her despair over the denial she witnessed concerning the threat of atomic annihilation and linked it to a distracted lifestyle that disavows responsibility for other's suffering. Her years of studying had taught her to honor the Buddhist belief that life is suffering and suffering for others is love. To connect with her own Christian faith, Veronica reopened herself to the cross of Christ through which God suffers with and for all people. She shared that in response to this call to suffering love, she had involved herself in the youth group and hoped to make new connections with each of the guys.

One night when only the youngest group members were present, I asked them what it meant to experience the presence of Christ. When the guys struggled to answer the question, I suggested that they take a moment to remember an experience from their past that they often replay in their minds. As the sharing began a thirteen-year-old African American leaned forward and said, "The experience I remember is my birthday party when I was three years old, when my Mom was dancing around me as I was blowing out the candles of a big cake she had set in front of me. She was wearing a birthday hat and carrying a present in her hands as she danced around." Struck by the detail of this young man's remembrance, I asked him to tell us more.

"So your Mom was dancing around you wearing a hat. What kind of hat was she wearing?"

He responded, "A birthday hat, a pointed one."

I then asked, "Do you have a photograph of yourself at this party?"

"No," he said.

Sensing that the memory held great significance, I struggled to remember what I knew about his parents. Remembering he was being raised by his adult brother. I asked, "Desmond, is your mother still alive?"

"No."

"How old were you when she passed?"

"Seven."

"How often do you think of this memory?"

"Every day."

With this response the air in the room seemed to disappear and together all of us were empathetically drawn into the emptiness that the death of Desmond's mother had left behind in him.

After a period of silence I thanked him for sharing and acknowledged the impact that this experience continued to have in his life. I then asked Veronica to share. After acknowledging the depth of Desmond's loss, she told the group about the day she met the Japanese poet Yasuhiko Shigemoto in Hiroshima, Japan. She shared that for seventy years this poet has been writing haikus that express the depth of emotion carried within survivors of the atomic blast. She shared how honored she felt to be in his presence. What she will never forget are the words he spoke to her. He said that her concern for the people of Hiroshima and her dedication to the anti-nuclear peace movement gave him hope for the future. Veronica ended by saying that even today the memory of this experience gives focus to her life.

After everyone present shared, I turned to Veronica and Desmond and said, "Just as you carry these experiences with you and they continue to play a powerful role in your life, so Jesus Christ carries your past experiences in him. He both holds them in the present and will take you and them into his future. The amazing promise is that what has not been right in your life will be made right in a new heaven and a new earth. There Veronica, you will meet Mr. Shigemoto again. You two will rejoice together and out of death and conflict you two, with God's help, will extend peace to the world that will last forever." Then to Desmond, whose eyes were already wide open with anticipation, I said, "You Desmond will be in your mother's presence again, and she will be dancing around you." After pausing a moment to get my composure I said, "You two can dance together."

In that moment a sense of the future made itself known in the room and the hope and peace that was present began to birth trust. We reassured Veronica and Desmond with invitations to remember Christ's resurrection and to receive the living hope that comes to us as ongoing gifts of the abiding love of the triune God. Through the outpouring of the Spirit of life upon all people through Jesus Christ, this living hope quickens our expectation that our lives will not end in death but will be gathered by the Father to abide in the triumph of God's life.

Moltmann explains, "Jesus has been raised from the dead and has become the Christ of the future . . . Where men and women perceive Christ's resurrection and begin to live within its horizon, they themselves will be born again to a living hope which reaches beyond death, and in living love will begin to experience eternal life in the fulfilled moment."[1] Moltmann invites all who perceive power in the resurrection to experience both "living hope" (1 Pet 1:3) and what he calls "living love" as the first tastes of eternal life in this world. For Moltmann the ability to perceive this eternal life is the ability both "to see through" to understanding and through to an experience of shared life "in God."[2]

We witnessed hope rising in Veronica and Desmond as they began to understand that the power of the resurrection was extended to them. It became a "living hope" as it served both as a marker of their own "faith in time" and of their "eternal origin."[3] As Veronica and Desmond acknowledged the power of hope within them, God opened the tri-unity of God's being to them, providing them an opportunity to taste eternal life. God's life-giving presence and love gave them the opportunity to experience traces of eternal life.

What Veronica and Desmond experienced was what Moltmann holds to be the fundamental truth about the resurrection of Christ from the dead, "in every end a new beginning lies

1. Moltmann, *In the End—the Beginning*, 164.
2. Ibid., 157.
3. Ibid., 164.

hidden."[4] What the resurrection promises is that the world will not find its end in death, but in God's resolve to create an eternal future. According to Moltmann the Bible does not contradict its own witness to the resurrection. The Son is raised from the dead by the Spirit of life whose power is greater than the power of sin and death. Through the crucified and risen Son the Spirit is sent out (John 15:26) not to secure a final victory through domination or violence but through God's love. God's life overcame death in the resurrection and will in the end overcome death in this world. The death of Jesus Christ, what Moltmann calls "Christ's hopeless end," became "his true beginning."[5] In the same way, Christ enables the hopeless to find their new beginning, the gift of eternal life.

The world will not be annihilated in a storm of fire, but everlasting life will be offered to every person, and then those who will receive it, together with the earth, will be transformed and become the dwelling place of God. Moltmann explains, "The future has nothing whatsoever to do with the end, whether it be the end of this life, the end of history, or the end of the world. Christian expectation is about the beginning: the beginning of true life, the beginning of God's kingdom, and the beginning of the new creation of all things into their enduring form."[6]

Wondrously embraced by the Triune God, Desmond and Veronica experienced the promise that "the one who began a good work among you will bring it to completion by the day of Jesus Christ" (Phil 1:6). Desmond was introduced to God's "living love" that met him in his grief and beckoned him to "approach the throne of grace with boldness, so that he may receive mercy and find grace to help in his time of need" (Heb 4:16). It is the living love, Jesus Christ, who shared and shares life with us and offers a destiny of everlasting life with God.

Veronica was offered "living hope" through the resurrection, which makes peace not by ending violence through violence.

4. Ibid., ix.
5. Ibid.
6. Ibid., ix–x.

Instead her attitudes and actions of suffering love are "aligned with the future of God's activities in the community of faith."[7] As Moltmann teaches, hope for peace rests in the indwelling of God in the people of his creation. While the power of God's surrendering love remains hidden and appears weak before the reign of violence and terror in the world, living hope rises in those who thirst for the righteousness of peace. It opens them to a deeper indwelling of God's life and love. Through sharing life with God and God's people, the community of faith is indwelt with God's reconciling love and fellowship, which makes for peace.[8] It is Moltmann's conclusion, "God's purpose in the creation of the world and in the covenant with Israel and the peoples [of the earth] is to make a cosmic temple in which he himself can live and come to rest. The 'Indwelling' . . . is the goal of all the creating, preserving, liberating, and redeeming in history."[9] Through such indwelling we are given birth into a living hope, which sets us free from vengeful feelings and empowers us "in the midst of strife, to bring conflict to a just end."[10]

When the Harriet Street youth group met a week later, there was a buzz in the air. It didn't take long for the conversation to be centered on the experience of the week before. While everyone present characterized the previous week's experience as uplifting, opinions varied as to what caused it. Again we took turns sharing our thoughts about our individual experiences. By the time we got to Desmond, the guys were using percentages to gauge either how sure they were about having experienced Jesus, or how ready they were to experience him now. When it was Desmond's turn to share, he did not clarify which question he was answering. He just threw both of his arms straight up in the air, rose to his feet and exclaimed, "100 percent!" When asked what he meant, he said, "I am 100 percent ready to experience Jesus."

7. Moltmann, *Ethics of Hope*, 128.

8. Ibid., 238–39.

9. Ibid., 150.

10. Ibid., 238.

While my mind questioned what outward actions should be taken, I felt myself partnered inwardly with what Paul called "the Spirit of Jesus Christ." Together with Christ and the Holy Spirit I was drawn to Desmond and felt great compassion for him. What was readily apparent was that he was no longer alone. In the midst of the experience, he knew who it was that companioned him and gave him hope—and I was a witness to it. Outwardly we prayed for Desmond and he reverently received our prayers. Inwardly my experience was of empathetically indwelling Desmond's need, being drawn into the Spirit's empathetic love, and then released with Christ and Desmond into a sense of joy.

Through what I now call indwelling prayer, many of those who were present that day personally witnessed the beginning of Desmond's relationship with God. Our group and a few men who were at church that evening gathered around, and I placed my hand upon Desmond's shoulder as we prayed. Sensing Desmond's vulnerability several of us prayed for God to fill up the empty spaces within him and to assure him of the coming reunion with his mother. As we prayed there was movement in the room and looking down upon Desmond I saw a woman's hand alighting on his shoulder with a feminine touch. Veronica had stepped forward and placed her hand on Desmond's shoulder. I sensed that the empty space left by his mother was indwelt by a woman's love. Veronica's willingness to step forward and to place her hand on Desmond's shoulder silently testified to a future union with God in which all people can participate. The peace and wholeness that Veronica had longed to share, now had begun to build community among a diverse group of people and was bringing healing into a young man's life.

Beckoned and drawn together by the love of God, the Harriet Street guys, their leaders, pastor, and all who prayed that night have a place within God's own story. Every person is indeed a hopeful story waiting to be told. Drawn into the wondrous embrace of God's hope and love, the believing community's view of the biblical narrative has changed. No longer does the Bible witness simply to possibilities; now it embodies opportunities. These opportunities are not initiated by those of faith but spring out of God's own participation in the sorrow, loss, and emptiness of people's lives. Every person is a hopeful story waiting to be told. Through the indwelling life and love of the Father, the Son, and the Holy Spirit, every person is an impending opportunity to receive ever-new life in and with God. First as hope and then as traces of fulfillment experienced in the life of the faith community, every believer's story begins to be told as an integral part of the story of the triune God.

Within every person God is welling up—through the resurrection of Christ—with hope in the midst of hopelessness. As God speaks in and through people's stories, God's immanence awakens God's purposes within them and they receive the gift of peace in the midst of internal and external strife. From the inside out, this peace draws every person into community, aligns each of them with those who suffer and awakens all to an expectation that the future is alive with the peace of God.

God's life encompasses everyone as an embrace of hopeful love, beckoning every person to allow his or her story to become a part of God's hopeful story. Held in the transcendence of God, people sense that in everything God is waiting to share with them the fulfillment of his eternal life. God's creative resolve continues to gather every person and to unite his or her story with God's own story. The promises of God will be fulfilled. In and around all of us, God continues to rescue the willing from the shadow of death, draw them into an eternal fellowship of love, and reveal their destiny to share in the new creation of all things. Those drawn by a living hope and a living love will be united in a single destiny in which Desmond will dance with his mother, Veronica will be a witness to lasting peace, and God will be the all in all.

Bibliography

Beker, J. Christiaan. *Paul the Apostle: The Triumph of God in Life and Thought.* Philadelphia: Fortress, 1980.

Manning, Brennan. *Ruthless Trust: The Ragamuffins Path to God.* San Francisco: Harper, 2000.

Moltmann, Jürgen. *A Broad Place: An Autobiography.* Translated by Margaret Kohl. Minneapolis: Fortress, 2008.

————. *The Church in the Power of the Spirit: A Contribution to Messianic Ecclesiology.* Translated by Margaret Kohl. London: SCM, 1977. 1st Fortress ed., with new preface. Minneapolis: Fortress, 1993.

————. *The Coming of God: Christian Eschatology.* Translated by Margaret Kohl. Minneapolis: Fortress, 1996.

————. *The Crucified God: The Cross of Christ as the Foundation and Criticism of Christian Theology.* Translated by R. A. Wilson and John Bowden. London: SCM, 1974. 1st Fortress ed., with new preface, translated by Margaret Kohl. Minneapolis: Fortress 1993.

————. *Ethics of Hope.* Translated by Margaret Kohl. Gütersloh: Gütersloher Verlagshaus, 2010. 1st Fortress ed. Minneapolis: Fortress, 2012.

————. *Experiences in Theology: Ways and Forms of Christian Theology.* Translated by Margaret Kohl. Minneapolis: Fortress, 2000.

————. *Experiences of God.* Translated by Margaret Kohl. London: SCM, 1980.

————. *The Experiment of Hope.* Edited and translated by M. Douglas Meeks. London: SCM, 1975.

————. *God in Creation: A New Theology of Creation and the Spirit of God.* Translated by Margaret Kohl. Gifford Lectures 1984–85. London: SCM, 1985. 1st Fortress ed. Minneapolis: Fortress, 1993.

————. *In the End—the Beginning: The Life of Hope.* Translated by Margaret Kohl. Minneapolis: Fortress, 2004.

————. *Science and Wisdom.* Translated by Margaret Kohl. Minneapolis: Fortress, 2003.

————. *The Source of Life: The Holy Spirit and the Theology of Life.* Translated by Margaret Kohl. London: SCM, 1997.

————. *The Spirit of Life: A Universal Affirmation.* Translated by Margaret Kohl. Minneapolis: Fortress, 1992.

————. *Sun of Righteousness, Arise! God's Future for Humanity and the Earth.* Translated by Margaret Kohl. Minneapolis: Fortress, 2010.

————. *Theology of Hope: On the Ground and the Implications of a Christian Eschatology.* Translated by J. W. Leitch. London: SCM, 1967. 1st Fortress ed., with new preface, translated by Margaret Kohl. Minneapolis: Fortress, 1993.

————. *The Trinity and the Kingdom: The Doctrine of God.* Translated by Margaret Kohl. London: SCM, 1981. 1st Fortress ed., with new preface. Minneapolis: Fortress, 1993.

————. *The Way of Jesus Christ: Christology in Messianic Dimensions.* Translated by Margaret Kohl. London: SCM, 1990. 1st Fortress ed. Minneapolis: Fortress, 1993.